The Professional Man's Money:

A Guide To Investment Profits With Questions And Answers

The Professional Man's Money:

A Guide To Investment Profits With Questions And Answers

Paul Preger, Jr.
David A. Loehwing

Prentice-Hall, Inc.   Englewood Cliffs, N.J.

Prentice-Hall International, Inc., *London*
Prentice-Hall of Australia, Pty. Ltd., *Sydney*
Prentice-Hall of Canada, Ltd., *Toronto*
Prentice-Hall of India Private Ltd., *New Delhi*
Prentice-Hall of Japan, Inc., *Tokyo*

This publication is designed to provide accurate and
authoritative information in regard to the subject matter
covered. It is sold with the understanding that the publisher
is not engaged in rendering legal, accounting or other professional
service. If legal advice or other expert assistance is required,
the services of a competent professional person should be sought.

*. . . From the Declaration of Principles jointly adopted by
a Committee of the American Bar Association and a Committee
of Publishers and Associations.*

Library of Congress Cataloging in Publication Data

Preger, Paul.
    The professional man's money: a guide to investment
profits with questions and answers.

    1. Investments. I. Loehwing, David A.,
joint author. II. Title.
HG4521.P77   332.6'78   73-4707
ISBN 0-13-725457-1

Printed in the United States of America

A Word from the Authors

From where we sit as financial writers, we get an excellent overview of the quality of most investment advice. Letters from readers, a great many of whom are doctors, engineers, and other professional men and women, describe the losses they have incurred by following the advice of an "expert." Some letters also mention sizable losses on mutual fund shares.

We are convinced that the individual who wants to invest—in stocks, bonds, mutual funds, commodities, or other areas—will be far better off in the long run to function as his own investment counselor. This book has been written with precisely that goal in mind. It is intended to help the professional man become his own portfolio manager.

Nor is it all that difficult to do. With a little study, anyone with the mental equipment necessary to become a doctor, lawyer, or engineer should have no problem learning the relatively simple techniques of security analysis which are described herein. What we have attempted to do is to leaven the instructive material with illustrative questions and answers taken from Paul Preger's column in *Medical World News*. Since the questions were actually sent in by professional men, the answers necessarily deal with very real problems that intelligent men encounter in their efforts to invest profitably and safely. Taken together with the straight expository matter, the questions and answers should provide a very practical guide through the securities markets, offering a basic, step-by-step procedure for selecting stocks and timing the purchases and sales for maximum profits.

To be sure, that's not all there is to successful investing. If all anyone needed to beat the stock market was to read a book and start plunging, we'd all be rich. Beggars would ride horses and financial writers would drive Cadillacs. The key ingredient, which only you can supply, is the mental attitude, the proper frame of mind.

Keeping Your Cool

If you can keep your cool and live a normal life while playing the market, you've won half the battle. The successful stock market trader has almost no fear of losing money. Indeed, he may have a healthy contempt for money. He is not afraid to risk it. People who are terrified of losing money never do well managing their own portfolio.

Your emotions are your own worst enemy in the stock market. It is fear—the strongest emotion—that makes people sell at the bottom of a bear market, and it is fear—of another sort—that makes people buy at the top of a bull market: fear that they will miss out on the easy ride their friends have been getting on the way up. Sometimes, of course, it is something even worse than fear: it is a drive to self-destruction, a wish to lose.

You absolutely must be able to be objective, detached, patient, and unflappable in your approach to the market. Otherwise you will never beat it. Furthermore, since the stock market is often both exciting and frightening at the same time, and because it occasionally really is a way to get rich quick with little effort, it can be addictive. We have seen people get "hooked" on it. They neglect their work, become irritable with their families, call their brokers every hour or two, follow the market's short-term ups and downs too closely, become terribly impatient when their stocks do not move up quickly, and end up doing all the wrong things at the wrong times.

If you are too easily worried, too emotionally involved in the idea of making or losing money, don't try to run your own portfolio. There's no point in getting yourself that worked up over profits and losses. It may sound paradoxical, but the first lesson for an investor to learn is that money is not so important.

Don't Follow the Crowd

The second lesson is to not be a crowd-follower. You've got to have an independent outlook without being obstinate. It's one thing to make up your own mind about the value of a stock and then buy it, but something else completely to hold on, come Hell or high water, when the thing is falling out of bed. One of the sagest pieces of advice given tyros in the stock market is: Don't fight the tape. Stocks will go down in bear markets, up in bull markets, and there's nothing you can do about it.

On the other hand, another equally sage piece of advice is that attributed to J. P. Morgan, who, when asked how to make money in the stock market, said, "Buy cheap and sell dear." The way to pull off that minor miracle, of course, is to buy at the bear market bottoms, when other people are selling in panic, and sell at the bull market tops, when everyone else exudes confidence. Such timing, obviously, requires a great deal of independent insight.

The Roller-Coaster Ride on Wall Street

Cyclical per se, the stock market is like a roller-coaster. About 70 percent of the time it goes up and about 30 percent of the time it goes down. When it goes up, it usually goes up much too high, and when it goes down, it goes too low. It seldom holds where it "should be."

As the roller-coaster starts upward on a long climb, most investors are very skeptical at first. But unlike the roller-coaster riders, they grow more confident as it gets higher and higher. When it finally reaches a peak that is far higher than anyone would have imagined earlier, almost everyone is bullish and looking for stocks to buy, just when they really should be selling.

As it starts downward, on what will be a long and devastating descent, the whole investment community is still highly optimistic about the market's future and about the economy in general. But as the downturn unfolds, investors become increasingly worried. Only much later, as stock prices go into their final rapid plunge to the bottom, do investors finally panic and become prophets of doom. That, of course, is the time to buy.

Faced with this seemingly perverse crowd psychology, as well as with all the evidence of insider manipulation and other abuses of recent years, the professional man with money to invest typically decides that he is too busy to manage his own portfolio, and he turns that responsibility over to someone else—the managers of mutual funds or bank common trust accounts, a broker, or an investment advisory service.

Some, contrariwise, continue to make their own investment decisions, but not on any rational basis. They follow tips from friends and associates, from brokers, from market letters and financial publications. Very few do their own technical or fundamental research. Unfortunately, the advice they get and the guidance they pay for is seldom as valuable or as competent as the professional services they themselves render as doctors, lawyers, professors, consulting engineers or whatever they happen to be.

The point is that the professional man, despite his superior intelligence and sophistication, often finds himself losing as much money in the stock market as the most amateurish odd-lotter. He really needs to take the trouble to find out how to be his own investment manager.

Some years ago, when we were working on the upper East Side of Manhattan, we would occasionally stop in at a nearby board room to check the market's pulse and sometimes make a trade or two. We began to notice that the brokers in the board room would often speak to each other, or to customers, in hushed, awed voices, about what "Max" was buying, or what "Max" was selling short. They would point to a large, heavy-set man of perhaps thirty, with black curly hair and thick glasses, sitting in the front row. "That's Max," they'd say. "He's fantastic. Everything he buys goes up, everything he sells goes down." Later, we discovered that Max was one of their biggest customers, such a good customer that they even gave him a desk in the front row, where he sat almost every day, apparently making money by the barrel.

The one person who really knew what he was doing was sitting there doing it, and wasn't telling anyone anything. All the others were giving out advice right and left.

It is our hope that this book will make a "Max" out of you, so you'll know what to do and won't have to listen to those who advise.

We would like to thank Dr. Robert T. Johnson of New York University, who is both an accountant and a petroleum engineer, for his material on oil drilling participation funds and other tax sheltered investments, which make up the bulk of Chapters 13 and 14.

We wish to thank *Medical World News* magazine for permission to use questions and answers which have also appeared in Mr. Preger's column, "Investment Q's & A's" in that magazine. Also, Figures 5-3, 5-4, 5-5, 5-14, 5-16 and 5-21 are courtesy of Trendline Division of Standard & Poor's Corp.; Figures 5-13, 5-15, 5-17, 5-18, 5-19 and 5-20 are courtesy of R. W. Mansfield; Figures 5-6, 5-7 and 5-8 were supplied by *Dental Management* magazine.

Paul Preger, Jr.
David A. Loehwing

TABLE OF CONTENTS

The Professional Man's Money:

A Guide To Investment Profits With Questions And Answers

1

HOW THE PROFESSIONAL MAN SHOULD PICK HIS BROKER

You are probably reading this book for one of two reasons: you have accumulated some money and are thinking of getting into the market for the first time; or, more likely, you've already been dabbling and are dissatisfied with the results. In the first case, you'll have to find a broker before you buy anything. That is a crucial step and merits consideration. In the second case, it is likely that your original choice of a broker is one of your problems, and it should be reconsidered.

Most people who play the market are customers of a broker they ended up with more or less by chance. He is someone you met at the country club, or is a member of your fraternal order. You read in the financial section of the paper that such-and-such brokerage house has done a research study on pharmaceutical stocks and you wrote in for it; one of their representatives called a few days later. Or, and this is the most likely, most dangerous reason, you heard of this fellow through a friend of a friend, and the rumor is that he's made wads of dough for a friend of the latter. That kind of rumor gets around because the broker has put his client into some wildly speculative situations that have paid off, temporarily. On the next dip in the market, the friend's friend is likely to lose his shirt, but you won't hear about that; people don't boast about having been taken for a ride.

The way to find a broker is to do a little research, and then shop around about the same way you would for a used car—suspiciously. Don't be afraid to kick the tires. But what qualities are you looking for? To answer that question, you first have to decide what kind of a market player you're going to be. Are you going to take the pains required to study it yourself and make your own decisions, or do you want someone to lead you by the hand and tell you what to buy or sell? We hope you're the first type, and if so, what you need in the way of a broker is an efficient clerk, who will expeditiously execute your orders but never give you a sales pitch.

His Own Interest Comes First

What you really have to understand about the stock brokerage business is that it is sometimes a conflict-of-interest proposition. The registered rep, who is probably the only man with whom you'll come into contact, professes to be looking out for your interests. It is certainly not in your interest to be constantly switching from one stock to another, but since he makes his money on commissions, he may have a tendency to get you to buy and sell more than you should.

In addition, you should know that brokerage houses are not in the business of buying and selling stocks only for their customers. Most of them are also underwriters, and play the stock market on their own account. And they usually do a good-sized institutional business, along with their "retail" volume, which is where you are pigeon-holed. In all of these varied activities, there are likely to be times when the interest of the retail customer does not coincide with that of the house.

Consider the underwriting business for a moment. A corporation decides that it needs to raise additional equity capital for one reason or another. The reasons may not always be the best, from the standpoint of the eventual shareholder: the firm may be over its head in debt, or insiders may be bailing out. In any case, it enlists the services of an underwriter, who leads it through the complicated maze of red tape called "registration," then buys up the new shares for resale to its customers—you. If the issue is of any considerable size, a syndicate of brokerage houses will be formed, each taking a specified number of shares for resale. Theoretically, of course, the underwriter tries to buy the shares from the company for the lowest possible price, and thus is acting in the best interest of his clients. Frequently, however, examination of the prospectus reveals that the underwriter is getting additional compensation, beyond his normal underwriter's discount, in the form of warrants or stock options. Isn't that a reward for pushing stock of dubious value, or which is priced too high, onto his customers? In any case, it's doubtful that the best interests of his clients are always uppermost in the mind of a broker who takes on an underwriting or joins a syndicate; more likely he has his eye on the underwriter's discount, which considerably increases his profit on every sale of stock to his clients.

Brokers also carry "inventories" of stocks which they believe to be good investments. Their research departments decide that a certain issue is likely to go up, so the firm buys up some thousands of shares for its own account. Then the research report is sent out to all the firm's customers, who in turn buy the stock from the inventory. But they don't necessarily get it at the price the firm paid for it; they buy "at the market." Here, again, the client is likely to get caught up in a conflict of interest situation. If the research department was right and the stock is going up, reps do not feel any great pressure to sell it to their clients. But when it peaks out, there might be a sales drive designed to lighten the inventory.

How the "Thundering Herd" Stampeded

Still another source of interest conflict may arise if a broker tries to curry favor with institutional clients. At latest count, about 60 percent of the trading on the New York Stock Exchange was on behalf of mutual funds, insurance companies, pension funds, etc., although they actually hold only about 40 percent of NYSE-listed shares. Because they buy in lots of 10,000 shares and more, their business is very profitable to brokers, who go to great lengths to get it. Individual clients have, on occasion, come out second best. Some years ago, the Securities and Exchange Commission brought an action against the nation's largest brokerage firm, Merrill Lynch, Pierce, Fenner and Smith, which illustrates the point. By virtue of his position on the board of directors of Douglas Aircraft, a Merrill Lynch executive learned that Douglas was in financial trouble. According to the SEC, the word on Douglas was quietly passed on to a number of large institutions, permitting them to sell their stock before the storm broke. Reportedly, some of Merrill Lynch's individual customers, all unaware, were buying. The same sort of thing reportedly happened to customers of another large firm when the Penn Central Railroad went bankrupt.

One of the worst things that an investor can do is to pick one of those relatively few customers' men who are intent on "churning" an account—the art of generating excessive activity in an account in order to augment commissions. A suit filed in New York district court against one brokerage firm shows how iniquitous the practice can be. A female client, the plaintiff, claimed that her broker, with whom, coincidentally, she was having a love affair, talked her into making over 1,400 trades in a period of 14 months. That cost her $122,000 in commissions and, since she was operating in a badly falling market, most of her fortune. The value of her holdings declined from over $600,000 to $6,500, at which point the firm froze her account, refusing to make any more trades on her behalf. The firm denied the charges, insisting that she was a compulsive trader and churned the account herself, against their advice. Whatever the merits of the complaint, the courts have, on occasion, found brokers guilty of churning. A California court, some years ago, awarded a Mrs. Bertha Hecht $296,000 in damages from one firm in a landmark churning case.

While churning is illegal and, as noted, brokers occasionally are penalized for engaging in the practice, it is difficult to prove if the account is not a discretionary one. For that matter, it is only in exceptionally flagrant cases that customers of brokers are able to recover losses which were due to the broker's double-dealing. A case in Milwaukee against Walston & Co. illustrates the point. One of the firm's reps there was found to have been exceptionally fond of Chris-Craft Industries; over a period of fifteen months, he succeeded in stashing away 210,000 shares in the portfolios of 51 of his 65 customers, although at the time the stock was declining in value. The 230 purchases were made at prices ranging downward from $10.50 per share to $5.50. As it happened, Chris-Craft was engaged in a proxy fight against dissident stockholders, and in a separate court action the company claimed that the broker had been illegally soliciting proxies on behalf of the dissidents. A Milwaukee court forced Walston to refund $25,000 in commissions to 47 of the broker's customers, on the grounds that he disregarded their investment objectives in selling them the stock. But nothing could be done about helping them to recoup their capital losses.

The Limited Protection Government Offers

Within limits, investors are now protected by the SIPC (Securities Investor Protection Corp.) against losses sustained when a broker goes bankrupt and can't pay cash balances left in his care or deliver stock certificates to his customers. In 1969 and 1970, dozens of Big Board member firms and even more over-the-counter brokers failed in a collective panic which, for a time, looked as though it might bring the whole Wall Street structure tumbling down. The problem stemmed, in part, from the severe market decline of that period, which eroded the value of securities the brokers were carrying in inventory and left them strapped for capital, and also from their over-expansion of the previous seven years, when brokers were setting up branch offices in every hamlet in the U.S. The chief difficulty, however, was the back-office crunch of those years, which burdened many firms with too many "fails." A fail occurs when a broker is unable, usually because of overloaded clerical facilities, to deliver the certificate of a security he has sold within the prescribed five days; it then becomes a charge against his own capital account. The NYSE and the SEC forced many firms to obtain additional capital and others to liquidate when they could not satisfy its requirement that debt be no more than twenty times equity capital (now fifteen times).

Although a $55 million contingency fund set up by the Big Board made good the losses of most member firm customers, it was touch and go as to whether it would cover all of them. Consequently, at the start of 1971, SIPC was set up with government backing to insure brokerage house accounts, just as the FDIC insures bank accounts. Customers' accounts now are guaranteed against losses up to $20,000 on cash balances and $50,000 on securities left in the firm's custody. Even so, customers of brokerage houses that close down may find themselves in a very uncomfortable situation. Consider, for example, the sorry plight of a client of First Devonshire, one of the 1970 bankrupts, whose account was frozen. It so happened that he held a short position in Polaroid at 58, and he had to sit by, unable to cover, while the stock ran up to 80.

When out shopping for a broker, therefore, one of the things to ask for is a copy of the firm's balance sheet. Since the 1970 debacle, virtually all major brokerage houses furnish them on request, regardless of whether they have stock of their own on the market. A firm that refuses to make audited figures available certainly is to be avoided. Nor is there any great difficulty about interpreting the figures. Usually, in the notes, there will be a sentence like this, from a statement of H. Hentz & Co.: "The independent computations made by the Auditors on October 31, 1971, indicated that the ratio of Aggregate Indebtedness to Net Capital was approximately 754 percent, as against the allowable maximum of 1,500 percent." Another way to check up is to buy the March issue of Finance Magazine every year. It carries a compilation of the capital positions of the 100 largest brokerage firms, with comparative figures on their fails.

Fees and Services

As of this writing, the question of commission rates is fairly academic unless most of your trades will be in the range of $300,000 and up. If so, you can haggle over the fees you will pay, as do the mutual funds and other institutions that buy and sell in such large volume. Otherwise, commissions are fixed. Anti-trust suits are pending, however, which may bring this state of affairs to an end. Meanwhile, if you expect to do any considerable amount of trading, it's possible to beat the game through a couple of small but reputable firms in New York, Source Equities and Odd Lots Securities, Ltd. Both offer commission rates about half as high as you will pay everywhere else. They provide no research, no recommendations, and no custodial service for your cash balances and stock certificates. When it comes down to it, that isn't a bad arrangement.

What do you want from your broker, then, if it's not tips and not custodial services? Mainly, you want an alert reporter, who will follow your stocks and keep you abreast of developments concerning them. Registered reps usually keep a handy reference file on all the stocks in which their customers have an interest, and they keep an eye peeled for anything unusual that happens concerning those issues. If there's a flurry of trading and the Consolidated Cathartic you're holding jumps three points in an hour, you should know about it; your broker should be watching the tape and call you when that happens. Similarly, if the broad tape (Dow Jones news service) carries a story that the FDA has posted a ban on distribution of one of the company's prime palliatives, he should be on the phone to you in a hurry.

Personally, he should be rather disagreeable and a poor golfer, so you won't get to like him and start taking his advice.

QUESTIONS AND ANSWERS

Q. What is the situation with regard to gangsterism in the securities market, and does it pose any risk for me as an individual investor?

A. Hundreds of millions of dollars are lost each year by pilferage from brokerage houses and from the mail. As an individual, you are now automatically insured for losses up to $50,000 on each account from brokerage house failure, fraud, and theft.

Q. My broker advised me to buy 300 shares of Murphy Industries for a short-term gain. I bought it at 16. Then the company came out with revised earnings which were down 39¢ per share. The stock fell to 11. Should I hold it? Should I blame my broker for poor advice?

A. The next time your broker recommends a stock, make sure he gives you a *compelling reason* why the stock should go up, and make sure the reason is very clear. Do not pay any attention to vague tips. And a professional man with a high income should be looking for *long-term,* not short-term, gains. If a broker doesn't know that much, he doesn't know much at all.

Q. What is the best way to find a good broker?

A. The same way you find a good plumber—talk to your friends and find out what their experience has been.

*Q. What do you consider the good and bad points of a total-responsibility invest-
ment organization—one that manages the entire portfolio on a continuing basis?*

A. The good points are that if they know what they are doing, they can make a lot of money for you and you don't have to do a thing, not even think about it. The bad feature is that if they don't know what they are doing—and some of them don't—they can lose a lot of money for you, and rather rapidly. If you think you have found a good one, try them out on a small scale first. Tell them that if they outperform all the market averages over the next 12 months, you will let them do it on a much larger scale from then on. A typical fee for investment management is 1% of the capital per year, or .25% quarterly.

*Q. I am now 65 and plan to retire in the near future. My portfolio contains five
mutual funds: Massachusetts Investors Trust, Massachusetts Investors Growth,
Investors Stock Fund, Chemical Fund, and Technology Fund. I also have about 20
individual securities. A security management company I have consulted recommends cashing in these mutual funds and investing the proceeds. They feel they can
bring me much greater growth and income than I am receiving. What do you advise?*

A. It depends on how skillful this particular investment management firm is. As a group, the funds you have should do approximately what the market as a whole does; these are large funds, and the law of averages will tend to manifest itself in how they act. Investment management firms sometimes outperform the market averages, sometimes do not. Some outperform them one year and not the next.

If the total amount involved is large you might consider a compromise tactic: keep *half* of the funds. And check to be sure the investment management firm you choose has a good, large research department.

*Q. Tired of paying high income taxes (my highest tax bracket was 48%), I
recently invested about one quarter of my funds in long-term tax-exempt municipal
and state bonds. Subsequently I asked a broker who knows my situation and he said
such investments were not for me. I am 72 years old and semi-retired. Did I make
a mistake and should I try to correct it or should I invest more in tax-exempt bonds?
I own an approximately equal amount of common stocks, and the rest is in savings
accounts.*

A. You seem to know what you're doing. The next time you hear the siren call of a tipster, stuff your ears with wax.

2

WHAT YOU SHOULD KNOW ABOUT MUTUAL FUNDS

If you own mutual fund shares, or if you plan to buy some later, the salesman probably has already told you all the good things there are to say about mutual funds. You should also be familiar with the bad things—the phony performance figures, the stock manipulation, the window-dressing techniques, and the gimmickry.

Even if you never plan to buy mutual fund shares, you should be familiar with the abuses because they affect so many stocks and mislead so many investors. The mutual fund industry has grown to enormous proportions. There are more than 500 of them selling their shares to the public, offering "diversification and professional management" to all comers. Their trading activities have had extraordinary effects on stock prices, for funds and other institutional investors tend to follow one another into and out of stocks, much like a stampede of rhinoceri.

When the fund managers get interested in a stock, they often bid for it very aggressively, pushing the price way up. When they become disenchanted, they proceed to dump thousands of shares on the market, pushing the price down so far that real bargains are sometimes created—for you. If you can see the stampede coming, you better do something about it, fast!

During the past decade, moreover, we have seen some investment practices by fund managers that would make a horseplayer cringe. As the mutual fund industry mushroomed in size, funds had to compete harder and harder for the investor's dollar. This meant doing everything conceivable to get quick performance results. Some of the "go-go" funds produced some spectacular net asset gains, while they were still very small in size and flexible. This made them the envy of more conservative portfolio managers, who soon got caught up in the same performance derby and abandoned their conservative ways. The result was a long period of heavy speculation, stock manipulation, and abuse, which reached its climax in the year 1968, as the great bull market of the fifties and sixties drew to a close with a classical speculative "blow-off."

Five Mutual Fund Abuses

ABUSE #1: Pushing Up Thin Issues

The compensation of mutual fund management is usually based on the total asset value of the stocks in the fund's portfolio. The greater the assets, the more money the management gets as compensation. It makes no difference whether the assets of the fund are invested in American Telephone and Telegraph or in a list of near-bankrupt companies that no one ever heard of. It is the size of the assets that counts. Accordingly, the sole aim of some fund managers has been to increase the size of the fund at any expense.

One way to do this, obviously, is to buy stocks that go up. As they go up, the total asset value of the fund goes up. If it goes up fast enough, the performance record of the fund will attract new investors—and the second way to make the total asset value go up is to get new investors to pour money into the fund.

In the 1960s, fund managers discovered what seemed like a very easy and foolproof way to buy stocks that go up. The trick is simply to look for issues in which the floating supply of stock is very thin. Once you have found a stock with a very thin float, all you have to do to make the stock go up is to buy more of it! With the supply thin, a slight increase in demand for the stock means higher prices.

Accordingly, the "go-go" fund managers spent all their research time looking for thin issues. If the issue had a glamorous name that suggested all kinds of growth and investment magic, so much the better. You could then even get other funds to join you in pushing the stock up.

In many instances, fund managers would keep on buying a thin issue, and keep on spreading glamourous stories about it, until the stock had risen 200 percent, 300 percent, even 1,000 percent above the price at which they first began buying it. The phenomenal rise in the stock would make a fund's net asset value go way up, especially if the fund were still small and owned very few stocks.

What made the fund manager's job even simpler was the fact that once he pushed up a thin issue, he never had to sell it. This was especially true if other funds had joined in the game. The rise in net asset value of all the funds involved attracted new fund buyers, so that new money poured into these funds at a rapid rate. This new money could be used partly to keep the thin issues from dropping back down—with just a few timely purchases—but mainly it was used to do the same thing all over again with another thin issue. While the individual investor usually sells, eventually, to take his profit, the fund manager who chases up thin issues never has to sell unless there are more redemptions than sales of his fund.

The game looked almost too good to be true, for a while—almost like proof that what goes up does *not* have to come down. But when the bull market finally ended and money became extremely tight, the thin issues started to fall of their own weight, and the funds lacked the cash inflow they needed to keep these issues up. Moreover, they had a hard time selling them because there were now very few buyers. The funds soon discovered that these issues were just as thin on the way down as they were on the way up, and to get rid of the stocks it was necessary to accept steep price concessions. As a result, many of the "go-go" funds experienced much sharper declines in net asset value, during the 1969–70 period, than did the more traditional funds that were invested in stocks of bigger corporations for which there was a more orderly market.

ABUSE #2: New Issues

This game is really just a variation of the thin issues game, because new issues are usually thin issues. The underwriters make sure of that. When new issues are hot, the average investor usually cannot get them at the issue price. He has to wait until trading has already started, and buy them in the after-market—at substantially higher prices. But mutual funds are the brokerage firms' most coveted customers. Their buy and sell orders are always "big ticket" items. So to please these big customers and to keep their business, the brokers make sure that the funds can get new issues, especially hot new issues. From the fund manager's point of view, the game is: you give us a big block of any of the promising new issues you can, and we'll give you lots of commission business.

During the 1960s, the new issues game was a way of achieving instant performance. The fund bought a block of a new issue at the issue price, and within hours afterward it had a profit that sometimes ranged as high as three or four hundred percent. Funds that relied heavily on new issues were hard hit in the 1969–70 market, when underwriters grew so cautious that they sharply restricted their underwriting of new issues. The whole new issues market calmed down to the point where instant performance was no longer possible except on the downside. However, the hot new issue game comes back to life periodically, and investors will see the funds chasing after these often-worthless securities again and again.

ABUSE #3: Lettered Stock

What could look better to a fund manager searching for instant performance than a block of stock he buys at 18 and promptly lists in his portfolio at 25? Lettered stock, or restricted stock, is often sold by a publicly-traded company to a private investor or mutual fund for a quick infusion of capital without the tedious underwriting process. The investor buys the block of stock at a discount from the market price, and agrees to hold it for a specified period (such as two years). But if a fund buys, say, a block of 10,000 shares of lettered stock at 18, and the same company's publicly-traded stock is selling at 25, the fund lists the stock in its portfolio at 25 and has achieved instant performance: a gain of 7 points on 10,000 shares. This sort of gimmick makes a fund's performance look very good. And again, the fund manager never really has to sell the stock unless his shareholders suddenly line up to redeem their shares for cash. What ruined this whole game, eventually, was the fact that so much of the lettered stock held by the funds was in highly-speculative companies whose publicly-traded stock went way down in the 1969–70 correction. However, this instant performance trick is by no means a thing of the past, and when you buy a mutual fund on the basis of its performance, you must check to make sure that lettered stock does not account for much of that performance record!

ABUSE #4: Squeezing the Shorts

This game gets a bit vicious, but it works, especially during a bull market. The fund managers keep their eyes on the short interest figures—the number of shares sold short in all listed stocks—published every month by the stock exchanges. When they find a stock with a heavy short interest and a relatively thin floating supply, they start buying it. As the buying pushes the price of the stock higher, the short sellers begin to worry. As more buying pushes it still higher, the shorts cover their positions in a panic reaction. The short covering, in turn, pushes the stock still higher, at which point the funds take their profit. Sound like fun?

ABUSE #5: Window Dressing

Mutual funds report to their shareholders every three months. At the end of each three-month period, they compute their net asset values per share and they list all their holdings. The report may be used by the salesmen to attract new shareholders, and it may also be the last straw that moves a shareholder to redeem his shares for cash. In other words, it has to look good.

Many of the purchases and sales made by the funds are made in the last few days of each quarter, solely for the purpose of improving the appearance of the quarterly report, and putting the fund's "best foot forward." If a stock in the fund's portfolio has dropped precipitously, the fund managers sometimes decide "not to be caught dead with it," so they sell it—dump it—even though it may have already declined to the point where it is a good buy. Similarly, if certain stocks have caught the public's fancy, the fund may buy these stocks in order to prove that they own all the hottest stocks, even though these issues may have already been bid up much too high.

Needless to say, all these window-dressing moves are made without regard to the shareholders' best interests. They are made in order to attract new shareholders and to discourage existing shareholders from redeeming. They are therefore included among the most common mutual fund abuses. When you consider a fund, it is not enough to look at the names of the stocks in the portfolio. You must also know when the fund bought the stock in order to determine how good the fund manager's investment judgment has been.

Even with Gimmicks, Performance Is Mediocre

Despite all these artificial methods of improving performance, the overall mutual fund performance record is not impressive—not even superficially impressive. For example, in a study of 330 funds, Standard & Poor's Corporation sought to determine how many of these funds were able to beat the market averages consistently. They compared the performance of each fund with the S & P index of 500 stocks, for each year from December 31, 1964 to December 31, 1969, and also for the first five months of 1970. They found that only two of the 330 funds beat the S & P 500 consistently— the Fidelity Fund and the Windsor Fund.

In a somewhat more comprehensive and long-range study, *Fundscope* magazine, which publishes all kinds of statistics on mutual funds, tabulated results of 428 mutual funds for the ten-year period, 1960 through 1969. Assuming an initial investment of $10,000 on January 1, 1960, with all dividends and capital gains distributions reinvested in fund shares over the ensuing ten years, the average liquidating value after ten years for all 428 funds studied was $21,255. By comparison, $10,000 left in a savings account for ten years, drawing compound interest of 5 percent a year, would be worth $16,436 ten years later.

While the average nest egg grew to $21,255 in ten years the best-performing fund, Fidelity Trend Fund, had a liquidating value of $51,344 after ten years, while the poorest performer during that period, Keystone B-1 (which, it should be stressed, was interested primarily in bonds and preferred stock), had a liquidating value of $11,475.

Of course, Fidelity Trend and Keystone B-1 are not really comparable, since the former invests only in growth stocks while the latter buys fixed income securities. But even within the growth stock category, liquidating values after ten years varied widely, from $14,611 to $51,344. The most speculative funds in the 1960s, the performance funds, which traded heavily and stressed thin issues and lettered stock, also had widely varying results. Liquidating values, ten years later, ranged from $49,866 for Enterprise Fund and $45,188 for Ivest, to $17,493 for Fund of America and $17,252 for Viking Growth.

These figures on ten-year performance, of course, include only those funds in existence for the full ten years or more. There have been many newer funds that actually lost as much as 50 percent of their net asset value per share by 1970. In these cases, an initial investment of $10,000 had a liquidation value of considerably less than $10,000 on December 31, 1969.

The important point to remember here is that whether or not you think mutual funds are a good thing, the particular fund you buy can make all the difference in the world. You can double your money in one fund, and in the same time span make only 10 percent in another, and perhaps even lose 20 percent in a third. *Mutual funds vary from one extreme to the other in their astuteness and performance, and you must therefore be highly selective when it comes to investing in mutual funds.*

The Case For and the Case Against Mutual Funds

The arguments in favor of buying mutual fund shares boil down to two main points: (1) You get the kind of broad diversification that would be impossible for an individual to get on his own, and (2) You get the advantages of professional management of the portfolio.

The arguments against buying mutual fund shares also boil down to two main points: (1) Diversification is not always desirable, especially during a declining market, when it only assures that you will participate in the decline, and (2) The portfolios may be managed by professionals, but some of these professionals are no better than the rankest amateur. A third objection sometimes raised is that many funds charge an 8½ percent "load" or sales charge, and this in effect means paying a premium for the portfolio.

Why do that when you can sometimes buy shares of a closed-end investment trust, which is essentially the same thing, at a discount? A tentative answer to this objection is that a growing number of funds do not charge a loading fee.

We maintain that mutual funds are strictly for people with no knowledge of or interest in the stock market, or no time to follow it. We suspect that any reasonably intelligent and interested individual who has enough time can learn to do at least as well with his own portfolio as the fund managers do. In fact, he can probably do better because he has several advantages over the fund manager: the amount of money he has to manage is smaller, the number of stocks he has to analyze is smaller, and he doesn't have to answer to a lot of impatient investors. Big funds are unwieldy and more difficult to handle. Moreover, they have to take big positions in the stocks they select. This means paying a higher price for a stock than the individual who just buys 100 shares. It also means accepting a lower price when selling. Finally, the fund has to buy many more stocks than the individual, thus increasing the chances of error and loss. Diversification sometimes reduces risk, but it just as often compounds risk, especially when the fund managers are incompetent. Over the long run, these factors should prove a decisive handicap for the big funds and make it more difficult for them to do as well as an individual or a smaller fund can do.

How to Tell a Good One from a Bad One

For those who do prefer putting some of their investment money into mutual funds, the big question is, which of the more than 500 available funds should I buy? The selection can make a tremendous difference in investment results, as we have seen.

In some respects, picking a mutual fund is like picking a winner at the race track. The only criterion you can go by is past performance. But even that is meaningless if fund management personnel changes every few years, as it does in some management groups. Furthermore, while horses tend to run "true to form" at least 35 percent of the time, in the case of the mutual fund performance derby, nobody knows exactly what *form* is. Funds are seldom consistent. The same fund will do well one year and very poorly the next. In *Fundscope's* study (mentioned earlier) of the ten-year results of 428 funds, it was found that *eleven of the 428 funds studied finished in the top 10 percent of the yearly performance race more often than once in the ten years covered by the study.* So, if a fund turns in a superior net asset gain one year, there is no reason to assume that it will do so the next year.

To add to the confusion, the comparisons become even more difficult when "dividends paid" and "stability during market declines" are also studied, along with gain in net asset value per share. Of the funds with the greatest capital gain performance, none was also among the top 10 percent for dividends paid. In other words, there is precious little consistency in the performance of mutual funds, and past performance is, therefore, not a reliable guide.

How, then, do you pick a mutual fund?

First of all, you don't pick one fund; you pick three or four. In this way you reduce the risk of having all your investments tied up with a loser, or a fund that does particularly poorly in any one year. You diversify, in other words, just as the funds themselves diversify. So, if you are putting, say, $3,000 a year into mutual funds, you put $1,000 into each of three funds, instead of $3,000 into one. Second, you choose funds with superior performance results *over a long period,* such as ten years, rather than funds that were sensations last year, and unheard of or nonexistent the year before last.

Third, you look, not only at the record of growth of net asset value per share, but also at dividend income and stability during market declines. Of the 428 funds covered in the Fundscope study, only 13 were found to be "above average" in all three categories of growth, dividend income, and stability during weak markets.

QUESTIONS AND ANSWERS

Q. How has the performance of closed-end investment trusts compared with that of open-end (mutual fund) trusts?

A. I do not think any generalization can be made, since both groups vary widely in their performance. Overall, I would have to call it a draw! There are certain times, however, when closed-end trusts—such as TriContinental Corp., Adams Express, Lehman, Madison, and Niagara Shares—are more attractive than mutual funds. This is when they sell at substantial discounts from net asset value per share. The discounts appear because the shares of a closed-end trust trade in the open market, like any other publicly-traded stock, and the price fluctuates with supply and demand. Largely by accident, sometimes, these shares may sell at discounts of 15% or 20% or more, for no valid reason. Mutual fund shares never sell at discounts because a mutual fund always stands ready to redeem its shares at the net asset value.

When the stock of an investment trust sells at a steep discount, the investor gets a double play. He gets a potential gain from the normal growth of the trust's portfolio, and he gets another potential gain from the eventual closing of the gap between price and net asset value per share.

Q. How do you feel about load vs. no-load funds?

A. I am more concerned with the fund's ability to perform than with whether there is the loading charge (usually 8½%). After all, a no-load fund is not a bargain if it only gains, say, 2% in net asset value per share while a load fund gains 22%. It is interesting to note that all 13 "above-average" funds previously mentioned are load funds. However, this does not mean that no-load funds are necessarily inferior performers. Moreover, the no-load funds have been getting more popular, especially since the 1969–70 bear market break made people wonder why they should pay an 8½% fee for the privilege of losing money. Many load funds may soon switch to a no-load status.

Q. I have been making regular quarterly purchases of a mutual fund sponsored by the broker I deal with. I am not satisfied with the way the fund has performed. In fact, the value of my investment is actually less than the amount of money I have put into the fund. I am thinking of selling the shares and switching to another fund. Can you make any suggestions?

A. Your situation results from putting all your eggs in one basket. In mutual fund investing, diversification is usually advisable. So, from here on, I would suggest putting your quarterly payments into three funds instead of one. Pick out three with good long-term records, and make sure they are different types of funds: one that is growth oriented, one, perhaps, that is a specialty fund, and one that is a balanced fund and has both common stocks and fixed-income securities. As to the shares you already own, I would suggest selling half of them and keeping the rest, just in case the fund begins to have better luck from here on (or better judgment).

3

MUTUAL FUND STRATEGIES
FOR THE PROFESSIONAL MAN

One of the experts who agrees that mutual fund performance is almost impossible to predict is a man who has made a smashing success predicting mutual fund performance. He is Pete Wurzburger, whose Hyperion Fund has substantially outperformed the market averages as well as the mutual fund averages. Hyperion Fund invests in other no-load mutual funds. That's all it invests in.

Theoretically, a fund that invests in other funds should be a good investment, since it involves professionals (hopefully) judging the performance of other professionals. In practice, of course, there remains the danger that when you invest in a multifund, you invest in two layers of professional incompetence—the management of the multifund, and the managements of the various funds it invests in. If both layers turn out to be as incompetent as some fund managers have been, you have a double play working against you.

Fortunately for Hyperion's stockholders, this has not been the case—at least not so far. From his old Colonial house office in Mt. Kisco, N.Y. (he got sick of commuting and subwaying to Wall Street), Pete Wurzburger uses some strategies that may be helpful to the professional man trying to pick out two or three mutual funds for his Keogh Plan, his professional corporation's profit-sharing or pension plan, his children's college fund, or what have you.

One of Wurzburger's overriding considerations is the size of the fund he may invest in. Usually, the list of the top twenty performers each year is heavily represented by lightweights—funds that are still very small. He also has to contend with the inevitable fact that when a small fund does very well, it invariably gets bigger, and when it gets too big, it doesn't do as well anymore. The sole exception to this rule has been the T. Rowe Price New Horizons Fund, which as a heavyweight $400 million fund was still outrunning most of the others in the performance derby. "It's like a 300 lb. woman winning the Miss America contest," says Wurzburger.

How does this fund's management do it? The answer, says Wurzburger, is that they take the trouble to know exactly what they are getting into. They do their homework. They have been particularly good at picking out small, emerging companies and good turnaround candidates, and sticking with the companies until they have very large capital gains on their stocks.

Trading the No-Loads

Hyperion's portfolio, at any given time, is likely to consist of about twenty no-load funds. There are currently over 130 such funds to choose from, so if Hyperion manages to choose a few of the best ones, without also choosing any of the worst ones, it will outperform the average of all funds, as well as the popular market averages, and consequently earn itself a management fee (which it otherwise does not take). Trading in no-load funds is obviously better than trying to trade in load funds, because you can get in and out of them without paying anybody a sales commission. In fact, trading no-loads is a good way of playing the market as a whole. When you see a big market move coming, you can participate in it through no-load funds with much more certainty than load funds, with their sales charges, or closed-end funds, with their prices that may or may not keep up with their net asset values. You know that when it comes time to sell you can always redeem a no-load fund at its net asset value.

Wurzburger and his associates keep a huge chart of the weekly performances of all the no-load funds they follow. The chart alerts them to trends early in the game. If they see a fund doing much better than the others, they promptly look into it, talk to the management, analyze the portfolio, and attempt to determine whether the superior performance in recent weeks was due to a fluke or gimmick or whether it was genuine. Sometimes it may be due to a run-up in one glamour stock in which the fund has a big position. That would *not* be a good omen. Or it may be the result of taking lettered stock and valuing it at the market price (see previous chapter). That would be a bad omen. On the other hand, the superior performance may be a reflection of price appreciation in many stocks in the fund's portfolio. That would be a good sign—an indication that somebody in the fund's management was picking and choosing well.

Once his multifund takes a position in a fund that looks like an emerging champion, Wurzburger keeps close track of what the fund does, but never tries to influence it or persuade it to invest in stocks that he himself likes.

Getting More Mileage Out of the Funds

The question asked most often by busy professional men is which mutual fund to buy. With more than 600 to choose from, including well over 130 no-load funds, how do you know which one is most certain to go up when you think the market is going to go up? And since the professional man is not, typically, a trader, how will he know which of the better performers is likely to continue to be a better performer, so that he will not have to sell it soon after he buys it?

Obviously a doctor in full-time practice cannot spend the time Wurzburger spends analyzing fund performance. There are, however, some simple strategies he can follow to get more mileage out of the mutual fund field than most people get. Here are the most obvious and important strategies:

(1) Buy several funds. Do not buy just one. This will minimize the risk of getting stuck with a poor performer while a good bull market is going on.

(2) Spread out your buying over a period of years, rather than taking the plunge all at once. This will minimize the risk of doing all your buying at a market top.

(3) Of the several funds you are buying, one should stress capital gain, one income and one a combination of the two. This will minimize the risk of putting all your money into a group of stocks that are about to go out of vogue (see next chapter, which discusses group movements).

(4) The performance fund should be a small one, since it is clear by now that the smallest funds have the best odds of out-performing the market averages on the way up.

(5) To choose a good fund, look at its record over a "round-trip market," that is, during a rising market *and* a subsequent falling market. If, during the up and down period combined, the fund outperformed the market averages and also outperformed the mutual fund averages by a good margin, then you can assume that the management of that fund does well in both kinds of market environments (bullish and bearish). Such a management should prove competent in the future. By using this criterion, you avoid the risk of putting your money into the hands of a group of managers that could do well in one special kind of market environment only.

(6) To evaluate your funds while you are holding them, all you really need in the way of data is the information in the back of the ordinary "stock guide" that every broker has and can give you. For more detailed "monitoring" of your funds, take a look at the last several issues of *Fundscope* magazine.

(7) If you are undecided whether or not to switch from one fund to another that looks like a better performer, you can always compromise by switching half of the money and leaving the rest where it is.

Faster Ways to Lose Money—or Make It

For the busy professional man who has neither the time nor the skill to look after his own investments, the mutual or closed-end investment fund is the usual, most generally accepted way of obtaining professional help, but there are plenty of others. You can put your money into a hedge fund or simply place it in the care of a professional investment adviser, usually in what is called a discretionary account. For that matter, most brokers will handle your money on a discretionary basis, i.e., with full power to buy and sell stocks for your account without consulting you. From what we've seen of the brokerage fraternity, though, it's probably not a good idea, unless you know one who inspires an extraordinary degree of confidence. There are also SBICs and venture capital companies.

The advertisement columns of the financial papers abound with offers of help from investment advisers, such as Spear & Staff or Danforth Associates, who take discretionary accounts of $5,000 or more. Their fees are based on the size of the account, so it is entirely in their interest to see your principal grow. Unlike many brokers, they are not likely to "churn" your account—make an excessive number of trades in order to earn higher commissions. Nor are they as likely to engage in the dubious practices of some mutual funds—window dressing, buying unregistered stock, etc. By comparison with the big mutual funds, they are small in size, so they do not face the difficulties of scale encountered by the funds. The other side of the coin, of course, is that, being relatively small, the quality of their "professional guidance" may be far below that of the mutual funds. Certainly, they cannot afford to pay high salaries to analysts. How their performance compares with mutual funds is impossible to determine; since accounts are segregated, supposedly with each one being given individual attention, the results achieved vary widely. With thousands of relatively small accounts to look after, it's doubtful that each one really gets a great deal of individual attention.

Some investment advisers accept accounts only in the $100,000-and-up range and limit the number of them to a dozen or so, in order to be able to give individual attention to each one. Frequently, their fees are based not on the size of the funds under management, but on the capital gains achieved. Here, presumably, is the "purest" form of investment counseling, yet the tales of woe recounted by investors who have placed their fortunes in the hands of such all-or-nothing advisers provide a sort of Greek chorus for Wall Street's never-ending tragedy. An adviser who gets paid only out of winnings inevitably is tempted to put his clients into the most speculative, go-for-broke stocks he can find. In a bull market he looks like a genius, but when the bear flag is run up at the corner of Broad and Wall, it's likely that his erstwhile boosters will get wiped out.

The hedge fund is another investment device which seems sound in theory but has bombed in practice. Hedge funds by the dozens sprang up in the late stages of the 1962–69 bull market, when it was apparent to the knowledgeable in Wall Street that the market was heading for a fall, but no one wanted to get out because the averages still were climbing. The idea, rational enough in itself, was to operate on a fully-invested basis, yet hedge the bet by shorting a few stocks which the speculators had driven to ridiculously high levels. If the market fell apart, winnings from the short sales would more than offset losses on those where the fund was still long. Fortunately, as it turned out, hedge funds were not sold to the general public, only to small groups of good-sized investors. Nevertheless, they were so unsuccessful that the hedge fund concept was thoroughly discredited—for the time being. It certainly will crop up again when future bull markets are nearing their tops. What happened was that the market upswing lasted longer than hedge fund managers anticipated, and they found themselves losing heavily on the stocks they shorted; they covered, then found themselves with no hedges in their portfolios when the market ultimately collapsed.

SBICs and Venture Capital Firms

For the most venturesome professional man, small business investment companies (SBICs) and their close relatives, the venture capital concerns, offer a valid investment alternative to the "go-go" mutual fund. They have a number of advantages:

—When it comes time to fill out your income tax form, any losses from an investment in the stock of an SBIC can be written off against ordinary income, up to a limit of $25,000 for a single person, or $50,000 for a married couple.

—Like closed end investment companies, stocks of both SBICs and venture capital companies normally sell at a substantial discount from net asset value. Especially in the early days of a bull market, therefore, they offer a means of "getting in" at a bargain price.

—Since, as a general rule, they are not trying to sell more stock and don't have to worry about redemptions, managements of these companies are not prone to the abuses common among managements of mutual funds—window dressing, etc.

—Both SBICs and venture capital companies tend to invest their funds in firms which are in the vanguard of technology. A breakthrough can bring fantastic returns. Moreover, their gains can be realized only if there is a public market for the equities of the portfolio concerns, so they tend to encourage stock flotations for those that are "ripe." In a rising market, this gives the investor a handle on what is likely to be a booming new issue market.

—SBICs have a good deal of leverage by virtue of their ability to borrow up to three times their capitalization from the government, at low interest rates.

The whole venture capital-SBIC movement dates back to the early 1950s, when directors of the venerable Massachusetts Investors Trust decided there was a need for companies that would provide equity capital for small new businesses; they set up American Research and Development Corp. in Boston to fill that need. Guided by a French investment genius, Gen. Georges Doriot, it prospered so mightily that it fostered a multi-billion-dollar government program, under the aegis of the Small Business Administration, to pursue the same ends. By the time ARD was absorbed by Textron in 1972, it had amassed assets of some $485 million, mostly in the shares of Digital Equipment Corp., which it had financed early in the EDP race. Original ARD investors, if they held on, probably realized a higher rate of return than those of any of the great glamour companies like IBM, Polaroid, or Xerox.

Chiefly to meet demands that it "do something for the small businessman," Congress set up the SBIC program in 1958 as a means of channeling investment money into small (assets under $5 million, net income less than $250,000) business. SBIC licensees could borrow twice (later three times) the amount of their equity capital from the SBA at rates only fractionally above the government's own borrowing cost. In turn, they were supposed to finance deserving small businesses. More than 700 SBICs were licensed to do business, and over the years they have put some $2 billion into client firms, but their numbers have diminished to about 280; some liquidated, while others, fed up with government restrictions and red tape, paid back their SBA loans and converted to straight venture capital companies. At latest count there were fourteen publicly-held SBICs and seven venture capital firms, the shares of which are traded in some volume.

None of the 21, to be sure, has compiled anything like the record of ARD, but the capital gains of a few compare favorably with the better mutual funds. In the eight years from 1962 to 1970, Capital Southwest approximately doubled its net asset value.

Westland Capital has approximately tripled, and Narragansett Capital shows a net yield on invested capital of better than 12.5 percent annually for ten years, compounded. In 1971, investors in Continental Capital received, as a dividend, the shares of a single portfolio company that were worth as much as they originally paid for their stock, yet they still held shares with a net asset value of double their initial input.

Of course, for every success story like the foregoing, there are a dozen failures that no one talks about. Over the years, no less than 75 SBICs have either gone into receivership or been forced into liquidation by the SBA; a number of company officials were sent to prison for misappropriation of funds. One of the largest of the group, Business Funds, Inc., was deeply involved in the financing of Westec Corp., a stock market high-flyer of the mid-'60s that fell to earth with a resounding thud. The president of Westec served a three-year prison term and the board chairman went away for five years.

Separating the sheep from the goats among SBICs and venture capital companies is a matter of looking at the record. It's reasonable to assume that managements that have been successful in the past will do well in the future. It's also fair to draw some conclusions about the quality of management from the business reputations of the men involved. For example, it is surely not sheer coincidence that Narragansett Capital is the largest of the SBICs and that its management team is headed by Royal Little, founder of Textron. The professional man who invests any considerable amount of money in this area should keep abreast of developments by subscribing to the market letter of S. M. Rubel & Co., 10 South La Salle St., Chicago, Illinois 60603.

In a bull market, stocks of SBICs and venture capital companies go up fast, but they go down even faster in a bear romp. They should be bought, therefore, when the investment climate is one of despair and sold when everyone is saying that prosperity is forever. In any case, if you're diversifying your holdings over several kinds of investment funds, only one out of four should be in this category.

QUESTIONS AND ANSWERS

Q. I am 35, have four children, and currently have ten thousand dollars in savings. I am now able to save about $400 a month from my practice after covering all expenses. I have no knowledge or interest in the stock market, but would like to invest my savings in order to be better able to pay for the children's college education beginning eight years from now. What steps would you suggest?

A. Since you have no interest in the stock market, and since you will probably be investing your savings a little at a time, you should plan on buying mutual fund shares on a regular basis, putting a fixed amount into several different funds every month or every quarter. As we saw in Chapter 2, mutual funds are by no means the best route to stock market profits. But you can minimize the risks involved by diversifying your investments among several different funds that have good ten-year performance records. And if you use the monthly dollar-cost averaging approach (a fixed amount invested each month or quarter) you will automatically be buying more shares when the market is down and fewer shares when it is up, thus lowering your average cost. With this approach, the odds are that your educational fund will be worth more eight or ten years from now than if you simply left it in the bank. The odds are heavily in favor of higher stock prices over a long period of time, such as a decade.

Q. Many doctors, and groups of doctors, have formed professional corporations which have pension funds. The doctors can contribute up to 25% of their income from the group practice to the pension fund, and this amount is tax sheltered. In your judgment, should these pension fund monies be invested in mutual funds? If so, what kinds of mutual funds?

A. I would suggest that your group pick out three mutual funds and put equal amounts of the pension fund money into each. You can repeat the procedure each year. The first fund should be one with a good long-term growth record, such as the T. R. Price New Horizons Fund or one of the Oppenheimer funds. The second should stress both growth and current income, such as the Decatur Income or the Puritan Income funds. The third could be a very high yield fund, such as one of the bond funds, since the pension fund does not have to pay an annual income tax on its dividend or interest income.

4

HOW TO REDUCE RISK IN A "ROLLER-COASTER" MARKET

Fashions come and go in the stock market, just as they do in women's clothes. One year the drug stocks are fashionable, and investors with their typical bandwagon psychology all pile into the drug stocks. The next year it may be the electronics or computer stocks, and the year after that it might be the paper or mining or bank stocks. At any given time there are "in" groups and "out" groups, and unless you are very patient, very lucky, or very skillful in digging out special situations and drastically undervalued situations, you will need to have stocks that are "in" in order to make money.

A dramatic example of group action is that of the airline stocks. For many years, these stocks did very little. Suddenly, in early 1963, they caught the attention of investors, and brokers began talking about them as "major growth stocks of the soaring 1960s." As their charts reveal, many airline stocks went up four-fold between early 1963 and early 1967. Then, for a period of slightly more than a year, they went into a tailspin that erased about half of the preceding gain. A relatively minor rally followed, and then came another drop to new lows, as the same brokers talked more about the airlines' cost-price squeeze than about growth prospects. The point to emphasize is that almost all the airline stocks traced the same roller-coaster pattern during the seven-year span in question. Traders who were aware of the group trend had the odds heavily in their favor by buying an airline stock in 1963, or even in 1965, and by selling it short in the middle of 1967 or in early 1969.

It should also be stressed that the extent of both the rise and the fall far exceeded the fluctuations in the market averages for the corresponding periods. Here, then, was an opportunity to play the market by riding along with a group that would outstrip the averages in both directions. Furthermore, it is obvious that the fundamentals of the air transport business, that is, the long-range outlook for profits, could not possibly have changed so drastically, or taken knowledgeable investors by surprise several times within seven years. Much of the fluctuation in the prices of airline stocks can therefore be attributed to changes in the mood of the crowd—in other words, changing fashions.

How to Stack Up the Odds in Your Favor

If you pick stocks out of a hat in a generally rising market, the odds are in your favor—usually by at least 60 to 40—that the stocks you pick will rise with the market. In a falling market, the odds are somewhat steeper than that, and of course, they are against you. So the first step in stacking the odds in your favor is to be reasonably certain that the whole market is in an uptrend when you buy or in a downtrend when you sell. The problem of identifying the market's primary trend is discussed in depth in Chapters 5, 6, and 8. But one point you should always remember is that the stock market has a lot of inertia. Once it starts going up, it keeps on going up until it is higher than anyone imagined it would go. And once it starts down, it keeps on falling until it has fallen lower than anyone might have predicted at its top.

So your chances of correctly identifying the market's trend are very good. You need only look at what has been happening in order to determine what probably will continue to happen!

I. *At any given moment, the odds are very high that the market will continue to do what it has been doing.* The same principle applies to almost any *group* of stocks within the market, such as all the steel stocks, or all the chemical stocks, or all the stocks of companies that are highly sensitive to changes in interest rates. A group that has been going up for many months will probably continue going up, particularly after a short-term consolidation or period of profit-taking has occurred.

II. *The odds are substantially in your favor if you buy a stock that is in a rising group which, in turn, is part of a rising market.*

A third rule of thumb can be quickly deduced from the first two:

III. *The odds are still better if you buy the leading company in a rising group in a rising market.* The reason for this, of course, is that you improve your chances of participating in the group strength when you pick the industry leader.

These three rules for stacking the odds in your favor are really just reflections of the way a crowd behaves in the stock market. Most crowds have a few leaders and several waves of followers. In the stock market, the smart money goes into a stock or group of stocks first. Then comes more money from the most alert and astute followers. Then the scene begins to fill up with more followers. Finally, as the last wave of sheep begin to climb on the bandwagon, the leaders of the crowd, with their smart money, begin to pull out. Slowly, the crowd begins to disperse and a downtrend gets underway.

The Danger of Buying Too Near the Top

The biggest risk in buying a stock in a group that has been strong is the risk of buying too late, or too near the top. The risk of buying at the top of a long move is greater than it might seem, because it is usually at speculative peaks that the biggest crowd of investors pour into a stock or stock group, under the influence of all kinds of wildly bullish appraisals by brokers and advisory services.

To avoid this risk, you must be aware of certain warning signals—warnings that a long-term uptrend might be getting dangerously close to its final peak. One such signal is a big increase in trading volume in the stock or group of stocks concerned, along with an increase in the number of brokers and services that are recommending purchase of the stocks. The result of all the recommendations and the flood of new buying is often a *buying climax*. Peak prices usually follow shortly after peak volume.

Another warning signal is the revelation that mutual funds have been buying the stock or stock group heavily for a considerable period of time. The funds report their transactions every three months, and publications such as *Barron's* often summarize what the funds have been doing. Naturally, the first few funds that buy a stock do well, but when a lot of other funds follow suit within a short space of time, a yellow light flashes for the professional man managing his own portfolio.

Most important, you should keep in mind the well-documented observation that when a stock hits its final peak, everybody is very bullish, enthusiastic, and optimistic about it. So one of the indications that a stock is still in a healthy uptrend is when a lot of people in the securities business and elsewhere are still skeptical about it. We can remember how skeptical everyone was about stocks like Control Data and Burroughs over a decade ago, when they began their long, steep ascents.

Some Mass Elimination Rules to Reduce Risk

Because stocks have always tended to move in groups in accordance with the sentiments of the great crowd of greedy or fearful investors, it is usually possible to reduce the overall risk of playing the stock market, and at the same time greatly simplify the problem of selecting stocks. This is done by eliminating from consideration whole categories of stocks.

Mass Elimination Rule #1

Avoid all stocks in groups that are in long-term downtrends. As suggested in the foregoing, if the group is going down, the odds are against any stock in the group going up. And when the group has gone down to the point where all the stocks in it look like real bargains, there is a good chance that it will go down still farther and take a long time to form a base and head upward again.

Mass Elimination Rule #2

Avoid all stocks that have been heavily exploited by speculators, even though they are not yet in downtrends. There can be some violent plunges when the speculators all decide it is time to bail out.

Mass Elimination Rule #3

Avoid all stocks that have been widely and unanimously touted by brokers and advisory services. Experience suggests that these stocks will not outperform the market averages. The very fact that everyone is bullish on them indicates that the buying has largely been completed already.

What Makes a Stock Glamourous?

A glamour stock is a stock that sells at a very high price/earnings ratio because the investment community is entranced with the company's products or services (often ignoring its financial condition or earnings) and feels that the company is operating in a field where sales and profits can grow rapidly. In the last two decades, a handful of stocks in such industry groups as data processing, office equipment, electronics, computer-related hardware, software, or services, and photography, earned the title of glamour stocks because they continually sold at inordinately high price/earnings ratios.

In the case of IBM, it is easy to understand how the stock commanded multiples of 40 or 50 throughout the 1950s and '60s. The company has dominated the whole computer field, a field that had tremendous growth potential, and the company's earnings grew by more than 25 percent a year on the average. Moreover, the earnings were conservatively-stated earnings. Computers, furthermore, have always mystified the average investor and this situation added further attraction to the stock. Even in 1970, when IBM finally broke down along with everything else, the stock was virtually a religion on Wall Street, and every mutual fund manager felt that his fund had to have some IBM in order to look attractive to potential investors.

In the case of Polaroid and Xerox, two other arch glamour stocks that have sported P/E multiples as high as 100 times earnings, it was a new product with wide appeal and wide practical application, as well as thorough patent protection, that did the trick. Xerox machines and Polaroid cameras were inventions that deeply impressed investment-minded people, and these two products each virtually became an industry of its own.

As was the case with IBM, both Polaroid and Xerox were able to report legitimate earnings that rose rapidly from year to year. The effect on investors, particularly institutional investors, was that they began to assume that earnings would continue to rise by 20 percent–30 percent or more annually, forever. The assumption was seldom questioned, and as a result, by 1969 both stocks still sold at more than 50 times earnings. Few people really believed that a day of reckoning was possible.

The key question, of course, is how do you pick out the glamour stocks of tomorrow? Which stocks, selling at 10–15 times earnings now, will sell at 40–50 times higher earnings two or three years from now? *The biggest profits come from stocks that the investment community re-evaluates at substantially higher P/E multiples.* This happens when investors are willing to pay more and more for each dollar of earnings—usually because they think the earnings are going to grow faster and faster. Example: Stock XYZ has been considered a relatively uninteresting company, and it sells at 9, while it earns about $1 a share. The P/E multiple is 9. Suddenly investors begin talking about the great potential of XYZ's products or services. XYZ's widgets can be used to reduce air pollution! Air pollution is one of the biggest problems of our time. It threatens to destroy all life on earth. XYZ is clearly a stock for our time!

Before another year goes by, investors are willing to pay 45 times earnings for XYZ. It is a stock that has been re-evaluated at a much higher P/E multiple. It now sells for 45. The investor who saw this coming has quintupled his money.

But how does an investor see it coming? The only honest answer is that you cannot predict what the glamour groups will be until they have *already begun* to take on a certain amount of glamour. If you understand how crowd psychology works in the marketplace and how the bandwagon effect unfolds, you can predict that XYZ, once it has already moved from 9 to 18, will go still higher. But you have to wait for it to go from 9 to 18 in order to be able to spot it as a potential glamour stock. Then, if you see the bubble forming, you can still more than double your money on the stock.

Investors could have predicted, and in some cases did predict, that IBM would go higher and higher, even after it was already "much too high" in the 1950s. They could have predicted, and in many cases did predict, that Xerox and Polaroid, despite their already high multiples in the early 1960s, would be accorded even higher multiples of even higher earnings a few years later.

Here again, we are back to one of the most basic principles of stock market behavior, namely, that once a trend is established, it tends to remain in force for a long time, until it has become completely exhausted. The glamourization of computer stocks lasted for well over a decade, giving investors a good long chance to realize that what had become glamourous would probably become still more glamourous before the investment world would see through the bubble.

Groups That Offer the Best Protection Against Inflation

Long-term inflation will probably never be stopped. The history of just about every currency in the world is one of steady long-term inflation.

Even if we did stop it, it would have to be allowed to start again very quickly, because the only practical way to handle the enormous, burgeoning federal, state, local and commercial debt is to allow inflation to proceed so that the debt can be paid off in cheaper dollars in the future. Otherwise, every time the government, at any level, borrowed money, it would be saddling future generations with an ever-growing burden of debt to pay off. This consideration, plus the more obvious fact that slowing inflation means slowing economic growth, and the fact that no wage-earner wants to receive less pay than he has been receiving and no businessman wants to receive lower prices for his products, suggests that inflation MUST continue, despite all the jawboning government has done about stopping inflation.

When the price of just about everything goes up, you can assume that the market value of just about everything that a corporation owns will also go up. At the same time, the relative weight of the corporation's long-term debt goes down. For these reasons, the stock of a corporation that owns a lot of things that go up in price along with inflation, and that has a sizeable long-term debt, and that has a relatively small number of employees (whose wages would go up with inflation, thus increasing the company's costs), *may* represent a hedge against inflation. In a sense, any company that is likely to keep on raising its dividends every year, or almost every year, also represents a hedge against inflation. There are scores of companies that have been increasing their dividend payouts almost every year for decades.

It is important to remember, however, that the stock market is essentially cyclical in nature. It does not move steadily upward, even when inflation moves steadily forward. Therefore, if you buy stocks near the top of a bull market cycle, no matter how many reasons you can find for regarding the stocks as inflation hedges, they will go down with the general market. To hedge yourself against inflation by buying stocks, you have to buy them as near as possible to the bottom of a bear market cycle or a correction, and *before* the industry group that the stock is part of has had a long rise on heavy volume.

QUESTIONS AND ANSWERS

Q. It seems to me that with the enormous pent-up demand for housing, and the virtually prohibitive costs of conventional building, the mobile home and modular home industries would be fertile fields for investment. Any suggestions?

A. You are quite right. The trouble is that too many people have thought of this already, and some of the stocks of companies with large stakes in these fields have already been bid up to rather high prices. A few larger corporations, including Boise Cascade, International Telephone & Telegraph, Certainteed, Kaufman & Broad, and Deltona, have gone into mobile and modular housing, and no doubt many others will join them shortly.

Q. In my naive and younger days (1955) I took a plunge into the Canadian penny-stock market and bought several hundred shares of Zenith Mines and Cameron Mines. The broker turned out to be a crook who sold only to Americans. About 1964, I asked a lawyer to try to find out something about this situation. He never really checked. I then asked a Canadian company to check, and I was informed that a court case was still pending. Whatever became of the two mining stocks? Are they completely worthless?

A. Penny stocks, like free advice, can be very expensive. I can't find any trace of Zenith Mines or Cameron Mines.

Q. A tremendous amount of spending is in prospect on pollution control and abatement. One figure I saw was $1.9 billion a year on controlling air pollution alone. Water pollution would call for even more than that. What stocks will benefit?

A. The trick is to find a company with a high percentage of its sales in some exclusive product or service related to pollution control. Four companies that Standard & Poor's *The Outlook* puts in this category are: American Bioculture ("Bio Chem" organic fertilizer); Marley (maker of water-cooling towers); Mogul (water treatment); and Trans Union (water and waste treatment). Other companies with specialties in this area include American Air Filter, Betz Labs, Buffalo Forge, Dorr Oliver, General Signal, Nalco Chemical, Peabody Gallion, Research Cottrell, U. S. Filter, and Wheelabrator. A great many large companies are, or will soon be, joining the fight against pollution, but in most cases the percentage of sales from this area will not be too significant.

Q. A major brokerage firm has recently recommended a number of newspaper stocks for purchase. I would like to hear your opinion on the industry's prospects from an investor's viewpoint.

A. Newspaper companies have a number of ways to make earnings grow, even when faced with sharply higher wage costs and newsprint costs. They can raise advertising rates a little every year because they usually have no competition; they can raise the cost of the daily paper, because it is, in most cases, still a bargain at 15¢; they will all be benefiting from technological improvements, including the automation of typesetting, engraving, printing, etc.; and if business picks up, they can get more ads.

5

HOW PROFESSIONAL MEN CAN USE CHARTS TO GAUGE THE PSYCHOLOGICAL CLIMATE OF THE MARKET

Basically there are two approaches to the stock market, the technical and the fundamental approach. Many professionals use both approaches at the same time. But it is also true that a very expert technician does not have to know anything about fundamentals, and a very expert and thorough fundamental analyst can disregard the technical picture and still do well.

The fundamental approach is concerned with value—with a company's earnings, asset value per share, the outlook for its industry, and so on. In other words, it is an attempt to place a value on a stock based on the underlying value of the company's business, assets, and earnings power. The object is to find a stock that is "worth" much more than it is selling for, on the assumption that sooner or later it will sell for what it is "worth."

The technical approach is concerned with the supply of and demand for a stock, and with trends. The technician studies charts showing stock price movements to determine whether a stock is in an uptrend, downtrend, or under accumulation or distribution. He is not concerned with the underlying asset value or earning power of the company. He may not even be concerned with what business the company is in. Instead, he plays a kind of game based on the market action of the stocks he follows. His basic assumption is that what the stock has been doing pricewise provides the best clue to what the stock will do from now on.

As a busy professional man managing your own portfolio, your best bet is to use both the fundamental and the technical approach, and to buy only those stocks that look good both on fundamentals and on the charts. Although it may seem more time-consuming to be concerned with both approaches, it is really much less so. If you were to rely on one approach alone, you would have to be far more thorough and far more persistent in your studies to make that one approach work. Using both approaches at once is actually a short-cut, because each one serves as a check on the other and thereby enables you to function on the basis of briefer research. Chapters 6 and 7 deal with the fundamental approach to buying and selling stocks. This chapter and the one preceding it deal with the technical approach.

Detecting Trends: Ripples, Waves, and Tides

The most important thing a stock chart reveals is the long-term trend of the price of the stock, or of a stock average such as the Dow Jones Industrial Average. In addition to revealing the long-term trend, some charts also show the intermediate-term trend and the short-term trend. These three trends can be thought of as *ripples, waves,* and *tides.* (See Figure 5-1.)

Since the ripples involve fluctuations that last no more than a month or two, and often only a matter of days, they are of no concern to the professional man, whose primary goal is long-term capital gains. The ripples are of interest to in-and-out traders, and to the "specialists" who make a market in the stocks.

For practical purposes, you should be concerned mainly with the tides. You should try to pick stocks that are in long-term uptrends, stocks where the tide is on the way up. The intermediate-term trend—the waves—are of interest also, but only to the extent that you will want to try to avoid buying near the top of a wave, even though the tide remains bullish. After all, why waste several months waiting for a downward wave to unfold. And why not try to buy near the bottom of a wave, when the price is lower? The waves generally last several months. The tides last longer—sometimes for many years.

To summarize, stocks and groups of stocks, as well as the entire stock market, tend to move up or down in long-term trends we choose to call tides, and within these tides there are upward and downward waves, and within the waves there are upward and downward ripples. Brokers who watch the ticker tape all day long, and full-time traders who jump in and out of stocks every day, tend to become preoccupied with the ripples, and have no patience with the waves and tides. You, as a professional man whose study of the stock market is, of necessity, only a part-time affair, should ignore the ripples, and try to exploit the waves and the tides. If you are very busy at your work, you can also plan to forget about the waves and concern yourself only with the tides.

Profiting from the Primary Trend

The biggest profits in the stock market—profits like the one your grandfather made, when he stepped off the boat and somebody sold him a few shares of Coca Cola early in this century, and he held them all these years—are made by riding out the tides. Even Shakespeare had something to say about this (not specifically about stocks, obviously, since there was no stock market then) when he wrote: "There is a tide in the affairs of men, which, taken at the flood, leads on to fortune." (Julius Caesar, Act IV, Scene 3) The fortunate long-term investors who bought stock at the bottom of down-

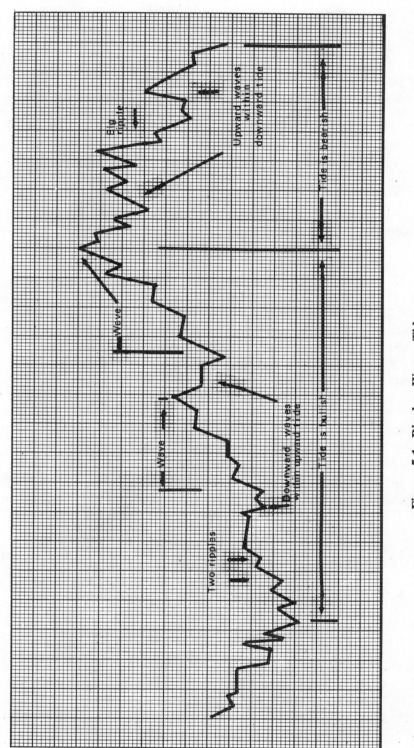

Figure 5-1. Ripples, Waves, Tides.

ward tidal waves, as for example in 1932 or 1939 or 1942 or 1949, and rode out the entire bull market tide that followed, reaped enormous percentage profits.

One of the most successful investment advisors, E. George Schaeffer, whose weekly market letter, *The Dow Theory Trader,* boasts a circulation of well over 50,000, based his entire approach to the stock market on the concept of riding out the tidal waves. In Schaeffer's view, *the simplest, safest, and most effective way for most investors to make profits in stocks is to buy a diversified list of stocks in a large number of different industries, at the beginning of a bull market tide, and hold them until the tide has unfolded itself in three large waves.* Then, he advises, sell everything and remain in a cash position until the ensuing bear market tide unfolds, also in three large waves.

Schaeffer was either very shrewd or very lucky in having launched his market letter in 1949, when the entire stock market was on the verge of history's longest and steepest bull market ever. In 1949, he set up two model portfolios for his clients and readers. Each represented a theoretical investment of $50,000. One portfolio consisted of a list of about thirty blue chip (investment-grade) stocks. The other consisted of an assortment of low-priced, speculative stocks.

Every week, beginning in 1949 and lasting until the spring of 1966, Schaeffer reminded his readers that the stock market was in a primary bull market, and that all stocks should be held. Even during the downward waves in 1957, 1960, and 1962, when most advisory services turned bearish, Schaeffer persisted in his long-range bullishness. He did not make switches in his model portfolios, but relied on the fact that they were sufficiently diversified to enable the investor to participate in the great groundswell of rising prices that characterized the whole 1949–66 period.

When this persistent Dow Theorist finally received a "Dow Theory sell signal," in April, 1966, and advised his clients to unload all their stocks and remain liquid (savings accounts, Treasury bills, short-term government notes, and the like) until further notice, each of the original $50,000 model portfolios was worth well over half a million dollars, after provision for federal income taxes on the long-term capital gains. The result was truly impressive, especially for the few clients who stuck to their guns and held everything until the bullish tide ran out. Figure 5-2 shows the price trend of the Dow Jones Industrial Average for the past five decades. The arrows show where Schaeffer became bullish and where he became bearish. Notice that he did not change his bullish stance during the many downward waves that were a part of the basic upward tide. Also, notice that the whole rise can be divided (with the help of a little imagination) into the three phases that Schaeffer claims are characteristic of all major tidal movements in the stock market (I, II, and III on the chart).

The Magic Number Three

If you plan to do your own technical analysis as a basis for selecting stocks to purchase or sell, the concept that every rise or decline of major proportions tends to have three phases will obviously come in very handy. Of course, it isn't foolproof, and if you go through a book of long-term stock charts, such as M. C. Horsey & Company's *The Stock Picture,* you will find many major rises and declines that do not have three

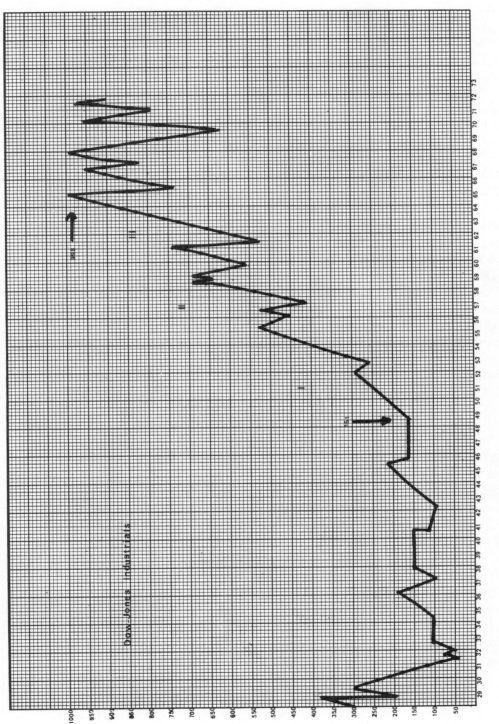

Figure 5-2. Dow Jones Industrial Average.

clearly identifiable phases. But by and large, big moves do tend to come in three's, so you will know enough not to buy a stock that has already had three big moves up. The odds are that such a stock is near the end of its rise and may have started a long-term decline. Similarly, if a stock has just completed three big waves downward, it may be ready for a major upward move.

Perhaps you are wondering whether this is just another numbers game. Why should a change in the price of a stock over a period of years come in three steps, or waves? Why not five, or ten? This is a valid question, but the only answer to it is, see for yourself. Look at the charts. You will find so many instances of three waves up or three waves down that you will accept the idea empirically. As for a rationale, one can only suppose that this is the way a crowd moves. It tends to get interested in a stock, or disillusioned with a stock, in three distinct steps. Something in the nature of a crowd accounts for this, but I doubt if anyone has ever explained the phenomenon in detail.

If Mr. Schaeffer's approach to investing interests you, you must be wondering how he got a "sell signal" in April, 1966. And was it a correct "sell signal?" Wouldn't the correct signal have flashed in December, 1968, when most stocks were higher, although the Dow Jones Industrial Average had not regained its February, 1966 peak?

While his clients—those who actually followed his advice after reading it—missed out on the whole speculative rise in lesser-known stocks in 1967 and 1968, they hardly have a right to complain, considering the gain in the value of their investments from a hypothetical $50,000 to over half a million. And they were lucky enough to be in a 100 percent cash position when the bear market started.

Beginning in the early 1960's, Schaeffer began warning his clients that the great bull market since 1949 had already completed two phases and was well into its third phase, and that a major bear market would develop when the third phase was completed. So, going into 1966, with the bear market long overdue in his mind, he was alert for the first sign of an important change in the tide. The sign that appeared in April was a classic Dow Theory sign, described by the late Clarence Dow, first editor of *The Wall Street Journal,* many decades ago. It consisted of a decline in both the industrial and rail average, a rally, and then a further decline, below the previous one, in *both* averages. This type of signal has proved to be false many times, and cannot be relied upon at all. But at the particular time Schaeffer took notice of it, the DJIA was still well up in the 900s, the bull market was seventeen years old, and Schaeffer was ready to change his tune, which had been bullish every week for seventeen years. So he sold out every stock in the model portfolios, and put all the theoretical money into cash or the equivalent. He advised his clients to put wax in their ears so that they would not hear all the bullish recommendations of brokers and other advisors. And he warned that the coming bear market would be a long one, because it followed history's longest bull market, and that it would have three distinct phases. As of late 1972, he was still warning that the worst (phase 3) was to come.

Figure 5-3

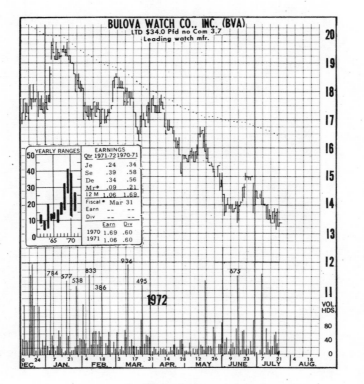

Figure 5-4

Picking Stocks from Charts

Here are three long-term charts. You can tell at a glance which one is clearly in a long-term uptrend, which is in a downtrend, and which appears to be trendless at the moment.

Three Patterns You Should Recognize

When you see a succession of rising tops and rising bottoms, as in Figure 5-3, you have a clearly defined upward trend. Since, as we have seen in Chapter 4, the chances are always in favor of a trend continuing at any given point in time, the chart should be regarded as bullish. If the company's fundamentals are also bullish, the stock is a buy.

When a stock is in a downtrend, as in Figure 5-4, the supply-demand balance for that stock is tipped over to the supply side. There is more stock for sale than for purchase, and more sellers than buyers. The stock will likely remain in a downtrend until the supply-demand balance finally tips over to the demand side. Figure 5-5 shows a condition without an apparent trend.

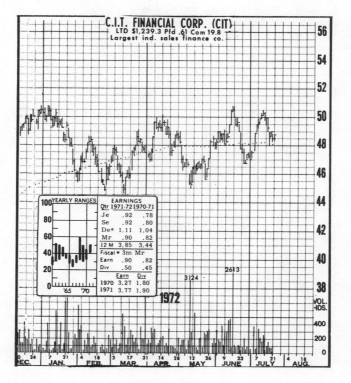

Figure 5-5

A change in supply and demand is usually accompanied by identifiable patterns on a chart that shows changes in price and volume over a period of time. Spot the pattern before it is completed and you can pick the stock near its low and expect a good percentage gain. Let's look at some of the more readily recognizable patterns that herald a change in the trend.

The Rounding Bottom

This pattern, illustrated in Figure 5-6, is frequently found in a stock that has completed a cycle of liquidation and is getting ready to start upward. It is often found among low-priced stocks. It represents a gradual shift from supply to demand. Notice

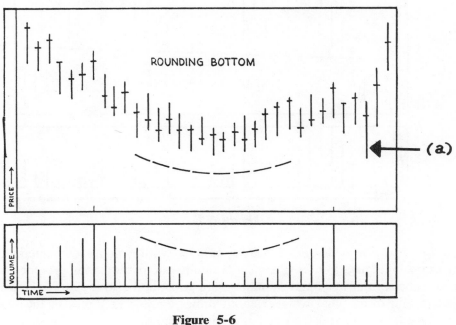

Figure 5-6

that the volume has slackened off as the bottom is reached. This suggests that the stock is largely sold out. The turnaround occurs on light volume, but as the uptrend gets under way, the volume begins to expand. A temporary sell-off at point (a) sends the price back down to the bottom, but it quickly bounces back, on light volume, to confirm that an uptrend is under way. As the uptrend continues, volume picks up again.

Head and Shoulders

This pattern is often detected at the top of a long rise, as the balance is shifting from demand to supply. Usually, when you see it in a stock you own, you should sell the stock.

Notice that volume is very heavy at the left shoulder. On the rally that forms the head it is much lighter, suggesting a drying up of buying interest. Volume is lighter still at the right shoulder rally. The third dip—from the right shoulder—drops below the "neckline," which is drawn across the bottoms on each side of the head. That is the sell signal, and often it is followed by a prolonged decline in the stock.

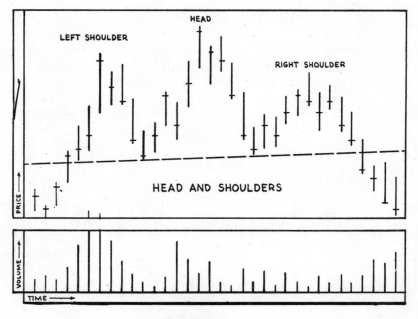

Figure 5-7

An upside-down head-and-shoulders pattern, with volume characteristics reversed from those in Figure 5-7, is often a bottoming-out pattern that precedes a long rise. In a way, the regular head-and-shoulders formation, and also the upside-down head-and-shoulders, illustrates what we said about things coming in threes in the stock market, for one is a triple top and the other is a triple bottom.

The Pennant

The pennant in Figure 5-8 is a triangular consolidation pattern within an uptrend. In other words, it is a wave within a tide, or a ripple within a wave. A line drawn through the bottoms converges with a line drawn through the tops. As we approach the apex of the sideward triangle, volume is low as profit-taking dries up. The advance is now ready to continue. The pennant represents a period of profit-taking within an upward move of much larger dimensions. As the uptrend resumes, you can usually buy the stock on the assumption that the next move will carry the price above the point *b* on the triangle, which means above the previous high.

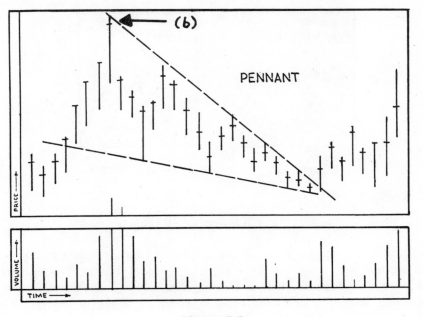

Figure 5-8

Other Common Patterns

Figures 5-9 and 5-10 show two favorable patterns, both suggesting higher prices to come.

Figures 5-11 and 5-12 show two unfavorable patterns, suggesting lower prices to come.

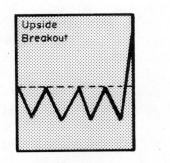

Figure 5-9

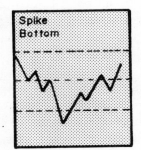

Figure 5-10

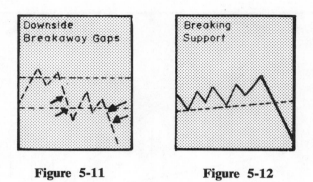

Figure 5-11   **Figure 5-12**

A Chartist at Work

As this chapter was being written, Steve Lipner, a chartist with a pretty good batting average as technical analyst for the Executive Capital Planning advisory service in New York, was consulted to pick out some charts that looked good to him and to explain why they looked good. Here are his selections, made in the fall of 1970 (see Figures 5-13 and 5-14). You can check the subsequent price histories of the stocks to see how good or bad Steve's choices were. Don't forget to allow for stock splits since then. The charts come from R. W. Mansfield's Stock Chart Service and Standard & Poor's Trendline charts. Where two charts are shown for the same stock, the idea is to give you a better perspective by showing a longer-term chart and an intermediate-term chart.

Concerning the charts of Searle, Steve notes that: (1) it is a drug stock, and at the time he made the selection, the whole drug group was a strong performer; (2) the relative strength line (see point *a* on Figure 5-13) shows a steady uptrend. This means that the stock's price performance with respect to that of the general market has been improving steadily; (3) the stock appears to be near the beginning of a major uptrend in Figure 5-14, which is a longer-term chart and which shows a lengthy period of consolidation between point *b* and point *c*. In Figure 5-13, moreover, the price has just risen above its previous high, which it recorded about a year earlier. Also note, in both figures, that at the low point of the whole consolidation (point *c* in Figure 5-14) the volume is low. This shows a low-volume turnaround, one of Steve's favorite bullish signs. Finally, the small insert *d* in Figure 5-14, showing a much longer price history (about thirteen years), indicates that the very long-term trend—the tide—is up, despite the decline from 1964 to 1970; (4) the runaway move from 34 to 50 (Figure 5-13) is a very steep ascent and suggests strong investment demand by long-term investors; (5) finally, Steve, who is strictly a chartist, says, "and don't overlook the A-plus rating in the lower right hand corner of Figure 5-13. This rating is the charting service's attempt to describe the "quality" of the investment.

The small numbers on the Mansfield chart at the tops and bottoms of short-term

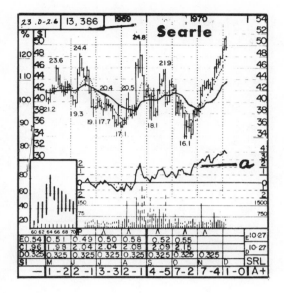

Figure 5-13. Courtesy of R. W. Mansfield

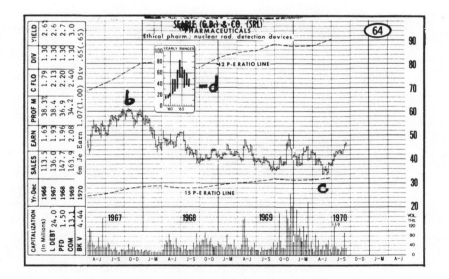

Figure 5-14. Courtesy of Trendline.

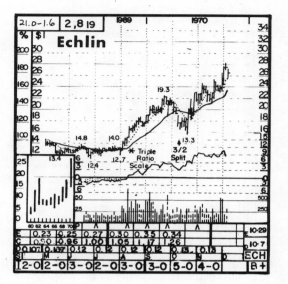

Figure 5-15

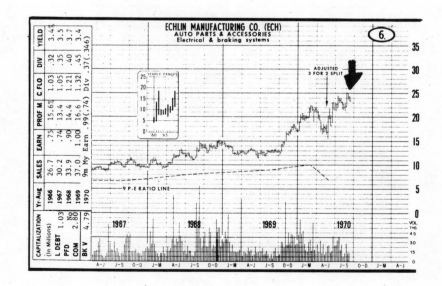

Figure 5-16

fluctuations are the price-earnings ratios at those prices. The numbers below the chart are quarterly earnings, annualized earnings, and quarterly dividends.

As to Echlin Manufacturing (see Figures 5-15 and 5-16), our chartist friend points to the persistence of the uptrends, both long-term and intermediate, and to the fact that the stock was actually rising, on a long-term basis, while the rest of the market was declining (see last quarter of 1969 and first quarter, 1970). "If you had this stock in your portfolio at the time these charts were published, you might have been well-advised to buy more and average up," says Steve. "This is a fine looking chart." (Subsequently the stock has been split.)

The Copeland Refrigeration chart, also an upward explosion pattern (see Figure 5-17), is particularly bullish because the stock is hitting new all-time highs while the rest of the market is only beginning to come back from its fall.

Usually, a stock that is hitting new highs is a good trading buy because the momentum

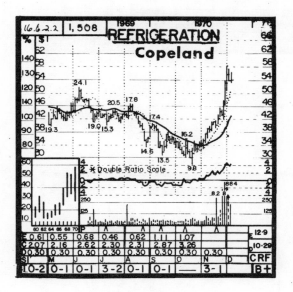

Figure 5-17

is clearly upward, and because the stockholders are all very happy and reluctant to sell their winner. With few holders selling, the bandwagon buying alone is enough to push the stock higher.

Here are some more stocks that looked to Steve as if they were ready to go higher (see Figures 5-18, 5-19, and 5-20). Notice that Coca Cola Bottling (of N.Y.) is hitting new highs easily; that Jantzen shows a rounded bottom on low volume; that Electronics Corp. has the rising "W" pattern.

Next, we have an entirely different kind of chart (Figure 5-21). This one shows the amount of uninvested cash in the hands of mutual funds, but the chart has been inverted so that it can be used as an indicator of mutual fund optimism or pessimism.

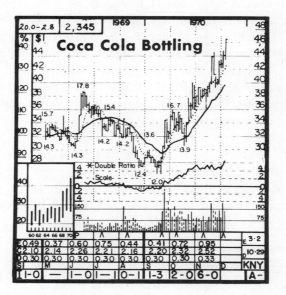

Figure 5-18

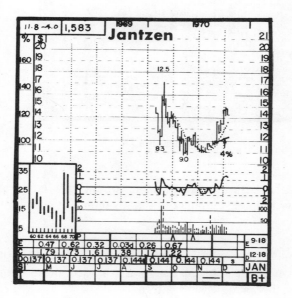

Figure 5-19

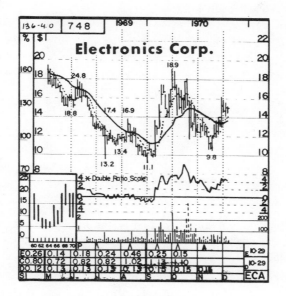

Figure 5-20

When the funds have a lot of cash, they are pessimistic. We learned in Chapter 3 that when everybody is pessimistic, that's a good time to be optimistic. As Steve says, "If you decide to follow the activity of, let's say, ten stock market losers, with the idea of acting opposite to them, you are thinking like a pro." Mutual fund managers are more likely to be losers than winners, judging from their past performance. This chart shows widespread pessimism about the future. This is an excellent reason to be optimistic. Note that the chart ends in the early summer of 1970.

Summing up his advice, Steve says that successful investors he has known put heavy emphasis on the six month to two year outlook. You should recognize that stock market reports, especially those on radio and television, and to a lesser extent those in the daily newspaper, work against your joining this select group. Stick to your own interpretation of the charts. "In the stock market, free advice is expensive."

QUESTIONS AND ANSWERS

Q. I bought McDonnell-Douglas at 20 in December. It is now in the mid-30s. How long should I keep it?

A. My favorite system is to sell *half* after a stock doubles! That way you get your money back and still have the same initial investment.

Q. How do you interpret a very high volume of trading? Is it a good or bad omen?

A. It means the pot is boiling and that in itself is not so good. But what is good is that whenever the market rises on both high-volume days and low-volume days,

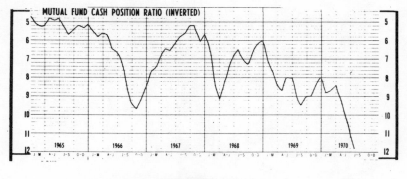

Figure 5-21

it suggests that whatever the volume of trading is, the market is able to go up. The very heavy trading is the result of mutual funds and other institutions making huge trades all over the place.

Q. How good are computers at picking stocks?

A. There are, at the present time, a number of services that claim to offer buy, hold, and sell recommendations that come from a computer. One thing a computer can do that "hand methods" cannot do is to screen thousands of stocks for a given set of characteristics, such as low price-earnings ratio, high book value, rising earnings, and so on. A computer can quickly find all the stocks that have the characteristics you are looking for, thereby performing the first screening step in selecting stocks for purchase or sale. Given the "rules," in other words, the computer can be complete, objective, and unprejudiced, and will get the job done without ever getting tired. Just how useful and profitable its recommendations are, and how reliable, depends entirely upon the people who program it.

If you are considering a computer-based advisory service, you should get from the service a good explanation of its rationale. Just what is it that the computer is screening for, and how are the computer print-outs handled for further screening and refinement? If the rationale sounds good, then you should try to find out what the service's track record has been. The proof of the pudding, after all, is in the eating. Finally, if you actually use such a service you should remember that a computer can deal only with measurable information. It deals only in quantities, not in qualities.

How good is a computer at picking stocks and forecasting economic trends? Every bit as good as the people who program it and interpret its output. No better, no worse.

Q. If one selected at random a portfolio of stocks that have been hitting new highs and another of stocks that have been hitting new lows, wouldn't the new highs' portfolio perform much better—and isn't that a good way to make profits in the stock market?

A. Over the near term, probability is that stocks hitting new highs will go higher still, due to the bandwagon effect. Likewise, those hitting new lows may go lower. Over the long term, the results would probably be as random as throwing darts at the financial page.

6

HOW TO REALIZE LONG-TERM GAINS THROUGH FUNDAMENTAL ANALYSIS

One of the authors had an experience with his first big winner in the stock market based largely on fundamental analysis, although he would be the first to admit that it is also partly a story of sheer luck.

One of the stocks that came way down during the 1957 market correction was Interstate Department Stores (now named Interstate Stores). At the time, he knew that the market's great tidal wave was upward, and it still had many years to go. So any stock that had a very big spill was a possible rebound play. Interstate had been as high as 60 and dropped all the way to the low 20's in 1957, after omitting a dividend and watching its profits melt away. The stock, moreover, had a book value of 50, a figure that roughly represented the underlying asset value of each share of stock.

Among the factors that interested him and certain other investors as they watched the stock over the next year or so was the fact that another retail company, the United Whelan Corporation, had just bought a large amount of the stock and was reportedly interested in getting control of the company. This meant that there was the possibility of a takeover at higher prices than the market price. Also interesting was Interstate's first experiment with discount retailing, which proved so encouraging to the company president, the now-famous Sol Cantor, that a decision was made to change the thrust of the company's business from an emphasis on conventional department stores to expansion into the discount department store business.

At that time the discount department store was still a relatively new phenomenon, but looked as though it would prove to be a basic change in the retailing field because of the rapid growth of suburban shopping centers. It was not, apparently, going to be just a flash in the pan. Moreover, existing discounters had been doing very well.

Interstate's first big move in the discount direction was its acquisition of the Los Angeles-based White Front Stores, a very profitable operation—a going concern that could be expanded.

Also of interest was the small float of less than half a million shares, which meant potential volatility. In 1959, one of your authors bought 200 shares of the stock at 33.

For over a year nothing happened, but he held the stock because he was sure the potential in the situation was above-average and the risk very minimal at that price. Suddenly, this little-known company electrified Wall Street by announcing a second major acquisition in the discount field—the acquisition of Topps Stores, an extensive chain, mainly in the midwestern states. Now the company's image was completely changed, from that of a stodgy conventional department store chain to that of a bold new enterprise in the glamourous discount field. The acquisition added immediately to earning power by something like 50 percent, and the company was suddenly a rapidly expanding business that would add new stores to the White Front and Topps Stores very rapidly.

In a matter of months the stock went from the 30's up to the 90's, as the combination of glamour and the thin float, and the prospect of sharply higher earnings per share, lit a fire under the situation. The author and the group of investors who had bought just before him congratulated themselves and took their profits—they in the 60's and 70's, the author in the 80's. Then, to add to their astonishment, the stock went straight up to 150 and was split three-for-one. In short, ISD was one of the top ten performers of 1961, which, it should be noted, was a year of very heavy speculation.

In 1962, the combined effect of the market break (740 to 525 on the Dow Jones Industrials) and a wave of bankruptcies among smaller discount operations battered the stock all the way back to 20 (the split shares). This was still almost triple the price at which the author first bought. But as the market recovery got underway and reports from the company indicated that earnings were indeed materializing as expected, and business was booming at all the new stores, he bought back in. The stock continued on its extraordinary ascent, reaching the 70's and splitting again. Here, too, he sold too soon, before the rise exhausted itself. Eventually, the stock reached a level which—counting all the splits and stock dividends—exceeded 14 times the price of his original purchase. But during the ensuing bear market, it dropped from 45 (which was about 450 on the old stock, before all the splits and stock dividends) down to almost nothing, as over-ambitious expansion and poor controls caught up with the company and began wreaking havoc with earnings.

Looking for the Fundamentals

Interstate Department Stores' meteoric rise between 1960 and 1968 is not the best example of what fundamental analysis can dig up, because there was really a lot of luck and happenstance involved. But there were certain key points that were attractive on a fundamental basis. These included: the high underlying asset value, the prospect of sharply rising earnings, and the entry into a field investors considered glamourous. Also intriguing were the very well-chosen acquisitions, which enabled the company to enter the new field without starting from scratch, and which immediately enhanced the earnings per share.

In essence, the fundamental analyst deals with three principal parameters: The price-earnings ratio, the trend of earnings per share, and the asset value per share, as compared with the market price. He looks for a low price-earnings ratio, earnings that are rising faster than those of the market averages (or will soon be doing so), and a possible asset play. In contrast to the technical analyst, who will often buy a stock that has just recorded a new high, the fundamental analyst is more likely to buy one that is lower than it has been in a long time. The fundamental analyst is also concerned with the outlook for the industry in which the company operates, and with the outlook for the entire economy. Usually he is a much longer-term investor than is the chartist, who often trades in and out of stocks without even waiting for the six-month capital gain period to unfold. Finally, the fundamentalist is more balance-sheet oriented than is the technician. He prefers a company with little or no long-term debt, and with a relatively high ratio of current assets to current liabilities. He likes profits that are predictable, and companies that are firmly entrenched in their fields and are basic to the U.S. economy.

The stock market is primarily a study in the behavior of crowds. What the stock market will do next depends heavily upon how crowds of greedy or fearful people will behave next, en masse. The collective delusions and impulses of these easily-swayed, materialistic crowds make stock prices go up or down, and thus the realities of human nature have more effect upon stock prices than the fundamentals of business. Nevertheless, fundamentals are important in selecting stocks that are most likely to participate in any mass move one sees developing. Whether the buyer is aware of it or not, every stock purchase, in the last analysis, is based on three questions:

(1) What will the earnings and dividends be on this stock in the future?

(2) What earnings and dividends are already discounted in the current price of the stock?

(3) Is there enough difference between (1) and (2) to make the risk of buying the stock worthwhile?

Rising Earnings

Most recommendations are made on the basis of rising earnings per share. Predictions of rising earnings, in turn, are based on rising sales, widening profit margins (higher selling prices or lower expenses) or both. If an automobile company will sell more automobiles next year, and still more the following year, earnings per share should go up. If a copper mining company can raise the price of primary copper, its earnings should go up. If a conglomerate company can get rid of a division that has been losing a lot of money, and the rest of the company is profitable, earnings should go up. All other things being equal, the prospect of improving earnings per share is one of the principal forces that can propel the price of a stock higher.

One fund manager who puts considerable emphasis on earnings per share uses these screening criteria in selecting stocks for his fund's portfolio:

(1) The company's earnings per share must be rising faster than earnings of the market averages.

(2) The probability of rising earnings must be confirmed by the fact that the stock

has already started to move higher. Uptrends usually last long enough so that you can miss the first few months and still do well.

(3) Only those companies that issue quarterly earnings should be considered. Without quarterly reports, earnings could stop rising and you would not know it for a long time. This criterion would eliminate many over-the-counter stocks.

(4) The rising earnings, ideally, should result from both rising sales and improving margins. But the investor need not be scared off by low margins, since there is always a lot of potential growth in the possibility that a company will be able to widen its margins.

The Price-Earnings Ratio

A stock selling at a price-earnings multiple of 10 can double if the earnings per share double. It can also double if investors decide that it is worth twenty times earnings instead of ten. But the important point is that it can quadruple if earnings double and the P/E doubles too. This combination of rising earnings and a rising P/E ratio has been responsible for the biggest profits in stocks.

Very often, the willingness of investors to pay a higher multiple of earnings for a stock is based on the fact that earnings have already started to improve. The rise in earnings tends to produce an assumption that earnings will continue to rise. If earnings will continue to rise, then the stock is worth more than ten or twelve times earnings per share. It may be worth eighteen or twenty times. This line of reasoning explains how a gain tends to feed on itself in the stock market, and how trends, once set in motion, tend to continue longer than you might expect. The combined effect of rising earnings per share and a rising earnings multiple helps explain the bandwagon effect referred to in previous chapters.

The close and continual relationship between stock market fluctuations and changes in the attitudes and emotions of crowds is most clearly illustrated by the manner in which price-earnings ratios have changed over the years. From a long-term point of view, the outlook for big business in America has always been favorable. It continues to be favorable. Thus from a fundamental point of view, that is, from a viewpoint based on the realities of business, the long-term outlook for stock prices has always been the same, namely, bullish. In spite of this, we have seen many wide fluctuations in the stock market as a whole, and many sharp changes of opinion as to what constitutes an attractive price-earnings ratio.

In 1949, for example, price-earnings ratios of five or six were quite common, even in the stocks of companies that were firmly entrenched in our economy and growing rapidly. On the other hand, in 1959, only ten years later, price-earnings ratios of thirty, forty, fifty, even a hundred, prevailed in many stocks. This fantastic change in attitude on the part of investors and traders was not based on the realities of business, because the outlook for business was clearly just as good in 1949 as it was in 1959. The change in attitude was purely a phenomenon of mob psychology. People had seen stock, both prices and earnings, going up very sharply for ten years, had gotten used to seeing this, and had begun to assume that it would continue indefinitely.

Even such a staid, conservative stock as American Telephone and Telegraph has been through some wide fluctuations in price-earnings ratios in recent years. The stock, earnings of which have increased almost every year over the past two decades, sold at a multiple of 12½ times earnings in 1958, at 24 times earnings in 1964, and was as low as 10 times earnings in mid-1970.

What Price Earnings?

While the price-earnings ratio, together with the trend in earnings per share, remains the most important single criterion of value to the fundamental analyst, growing emphasis is being placed now on the "quality of earnings." There are numerous situations where ten times earnings can be too high and fifteen times earnings can be too low. Here are just a few examples, without getting too far into technicalities of accounting:

(1) An investor notices that Stock A is selling at six times earnings for the year ended last December 31, and all indications are the earnings for the current year will be just as good. He finds a copy of the company's annual report in his broker's library, and looks at the income statement. Now he sees why the stock is selling at only six times earnings. The company paid no taxes last year, because of a substantial tax-loss in the two previous years. This means, in effect, that the multiple of six is really like a multiple of pre-tax earnings. Were the earnings taxed at the usual rate of, say, 48 percent, they would be about half of what they were, and the multiple would be about twelve instead of six. As soon as the tax-loss credit is used up, this is just what will happen.

(2) Stock B sells at eight times earnings. The company's principal business is the mining of non-ferrous metals. The company president has stated publicly that earnings will even be better this year than last. The investor again visits his broker's library and asks for Company B's annual report. Reading through the introductory portion, he notices that the company has a major property in a South American country. Over a third of the company's earnings come from the South American mine. Recalling the many recent instances of expropriation and nationalization of U.S.-owned properties abroad—such as in Chile, and earlier in Cuba—he realizes that earnings that come from South America are of "poor quality" to say the least. They could disappear any minute. So the stock is no bargain despite the low P/E.

(3) Company C, on the other hand, has been recommended to the investor because of the "high quality" of its earnings. The stock sells for 23, and earnings for the most recent twelve month period were $1.40. A projection of $1.55 is made for the next twelve months. This doesn't sound particularly interesting, since the P/E is fifteen (on projected earnings) and the apparent growth rate in earnings is about 10 percent. That seems too much like an average situation, but just out of curiosity the investor looks at the annual report. One of the first things he notices is the very large amount of deprecia-tion charges. When these are added to earnings, the result is a *cash flow* of $4.40 a share. On top of this, the company has no long-term debt, and no preferred stock ahead of the

common stock. Moreover, the company sees its markets growing and plans a substantial expansion program, all of which is to be financed out of its cash flow, with no need for any borrowing. Under these circumstances, with no debt and with the stock selling at less than six times the cash flow per share (earnings plus depreciation), the stock seems very cheap and may be a good long-term buy. At some point, the cash flow will be translated into higher earnings, and when the expansion program materializes, the company will be much bigger without having borrowed a cent.

In other words, there are situations where earnings per share do not tell the whole story. But on the whole, the P/E is the best yardstick. Generally speaking, a P/E of fifteen or less for a company whose earnings are growing by 10 percent a year or more is attractive. For a company whose earnings are standing still or shrinking, fifteen would be high. For a financially strong company whose earnings per share are increasing by more than 15 percent annually and are expected to continue growing at that rate, P/Es of twenty or thirty or more have been quite common and in some cases have proven justified.

The Asset Play

We have already mentioned one type of asset play in Chapter 2—the situation where a closed-end investment trust is selling at a significant discount from its net asset value. Unless there is something radically wrong with the investment trust, sooner or later the gap between net asset value per share and price per share will narrow, and this narrowing represents your profit. In the early 1950s, closed-end trusts sold at discounts of 25 percent, typically. By the late 1960s, they were selling at about net asset value, and in some cases at a slight premium. The person who held closed-end shares during those years not only received the benefit of the fund's participation in a broad bull market, but also the capital gain from the narrowing of the discount.

A more interesting type of asset play is illustrated by a situation that developed late in 1970 in the stock of Cowles Communications, Inc. Cowles stock had come down to about 4 largely because its principal business, *Look* magazine, was losing an enormous sum in 1970. However, the company had other assets, including TV stations and newspapers, as well as a substantial amount of cash.

Suddenly, a deal was announced which will probably go down in history as one of the best corporate financial deals ever. Cowles and the New York Times Company announced an agreement under which Cowles would sell the *Times* its three Florida daily newspapers and its Memphis TV stations, its medical and dental periodicals and an educational book company for 2.6 million shares of *Times* stock. Part of the agreement was that the Times would take over Cowles' $15 million long-term debt.

Since there were about 3.9 million shares of Cowles outstanding, the result of the deal would be that every share of Cowles would have behind it about two-thirds of a share of The New York Times Company. Shortly after the deal was announced, Cowles was selling at 6 and the *Times* was selling for around 20. This, then, was the asset play: a $6 stock with over $13 of *Times* stock behind it, as well as other assets, including *Look* magazine, which was losing money.

Over the ensuing weeks, Cowles stock rose very slowly but steadily. There was still a lot of skepticism: some observers feared that continued losses from *Look* would eat into all the other assets and earnings, including dividends from the 2.6 million *Times* shares. But for investors looking for an asset play, the salient point was the huge spread between the price of Cowles and its asset value once the deal went through.

Financial Analysis: A Glowing Example

One of the best ways to see what faundamental analysis consists of is to examine a report based on a thorough analysis. The summary of a report that follows was prepared by analysts at David J. Greene & Co. in September, 1969. At that time, American District Telegraph was selling at 23. Read the summary and conclusion, and you will get a good idea of what sophisticated securities research involves. (Two years later the stock hit 68!)

*AMERICAN DISTRICT TELEGRAPH **

American District Telegraph (ADT) is the dominant company in the central station protective service industry. As such, it is a major factor in the growing fields of crime and fire prevention and detection. On September 23, 1969, its shares will be listed on the New York Stock Exchange. This should lead to greater investor interest in the company which, although in business for 98 years, has been publicly owned for less than two.

Prior to January 1968, ADT was 80% owned by the Grinnell Corporation. However, Grinnell was forced to divest its ADT shares via a spin-off to stockholders. Such action was in compliance with a Supreme Court ruling that Grinnell and its Alarm Companies (ADT, Holmes and Automatic Fire Alarm) had violated the anti-trust laws by monopolizing the accredited central station protective service industry.

We believe that during the period of Grinnell's domination ADT's operations were inhibited by ultra-conservative policies, as well as by its preoccupation with the anti-trust action. We expect that in the future ADT should be a far more dynamic organization and better capable of capitalizing on its potentials.

We consider ADT's shares to be an attractive investment opportunity for the following major reasons:

> *(Note that the report lists nine very specific reasons why the stock is likely to go higher. How many times have you bought a stock and identified nine reasons why it was a good buy? Moreover, these are all compelling reasons.)*

(1) Spurred by the rising incidence of crime and fire, the entire protective service industry appears to be on the verge of accelerated growth.

(2) ADT has a nationwide network of 135 central stations serving subscribers in 121 cities throughout the U.S. and Canada. In our judgment, it has the facilities and specialized know-how developed through years of experience to participate fully in the growth of the industry.

* Reprinted by permission of David J. Greene & Co.

(3) Due to the nature and the rental characteristics of the business, ADT's revenues are recurring and virtually recession-proof. Consequently, its earnings and cash flow are of high quality.

(4) Because of a sharp rise in operating costs without compensating rate increases, ADT's earnings have been on a plateau of about $6.2 million, or $1.20 per share, for the past three years (1969 included). However, with recently initiated rate increases beginning to take hold, coupled with strong demand for its services, we expect a major upturn in profits to begin in 1970 with earnings estimated at $1.35 per share.

(Note that the above projection was (probably deliberately) on the conservative side. Actual reported 1970 earnings were $1.47 a share.)

(5) We estimate that ADT's cash flow, which is substantially greater than reported net income, should be about $22 million, or $4.15 per share in 1969. Because cash flow represents such an unusually large percentage of revenues (24.6% in 1968), we believe it to be a more significant figure than reported earnings in evaluating the company's financial results.

(6) Capital expenditures during the five-year period 1964–1968 totaled $93.5 million and should amount to about $23.5 million in 1969. These funds are primarily invested in new facilities, thereby continuously enlarging the company's earnings base.

(7) Based upon a capital investment program estimated to exceed $100 million during the next five years, we believe profits should grow by at least 10% per annum.

(8) In view of ADT's substantial, recurring cash flow, the company has a revolving fund to continually finance its expansion program without the need to sell common stock.

(9) ADT has no debt or preferred stock ahead of its common equity represented by 5,270,300 shares.

At the present time, the shares of W. J. Burns International Detective Agency, Inc., Pinkerton's, Inc., Baker Industries and Wackenhut Corp., which are smaller companies engaged in various aspects of the protective service industry, are selling at price-to-estimated 1969 earnings ratios ranging from 31 to 44 times, compared to 19 times for ADT. However, in view of the rental nature of ADT's business and the magnitude of its cash flow in relation to its net income and revenues, we believe that cash flow is a far more meaningful measure of ADT's investment value. Notwithstanding the fact that ADT's ratio of cash flow to revenue exceeds that of the above four companies, they sell at price-to-cash flow ratios ranging from 14 to 43 times, compared with 6 times for ADT.

(As we have seen earlier in this chapter, there are some instances where earnings per share do not tell the story. This is one of them, and cash flow, in this example, is a key factor in illustrating how undervalued the stock was at 23.)

As the major company in the protective service field, we believe that ADT's shares are undervalued and should sell more in line with other companies in the industry. Moreover, based upon the company's large potential and the quality of its earnings and cash flow, the shares in time could command a premium.

In our opinion, ADT at its current market price represents an attractive growth investment and purchase is recommended.

QUESTIONS AND ANSWERS

Q. How much of my funds should be in stocks, how much in bonds, and how much in a savings bank? I am a 45-year-old physician with three children in school and my income from private practice is about $60,000 annually. I own my own house.

A. Most of the time you should probably have half of your funds in common stocks. Most of the rest should go into tax-exempt state or municipal bonds because of your tax bracket. The only time I would suggest having much more of your funds in common stocks is after there has been a period of panic selling, such as October, 1962, or October, 1966, or May, 1970. These were all periods when investors were being hit by all kinds of dreadful national, international, and monetary news, after a long decline had already driven down the price of most investment grade stocks to bargain levels. At such times you can step in and buy stocks that are often extremely undervalued because everyone else is selling in a panic, and you will have substantial profits a short time afterwards.

The only time I would say that most of your funds should be out of the stock market is after a period of heavy speculation has unfolded, such as the speculative orgies of 1961 and 1968, when all kinds of abuses were taking place. It requires a level head to avoid being caught up in these speculative sprees, because they occur when nearly everyone is bullish and the one or two bearish voices around almost sound foolish.

Q. Are stocks really a hedge against inflation?

A. Some stocks are hedges against inflation *some of the time*. Between December, 1968 and June, 1970, inflation nibbled away at the dollar at an annual rate of at least 6%. During the same 18-month period, the Dow Jones Industrial Average dropped over 30%. Some stocks dropped 80–90%. For someone who bought a diversified number of stocks in 1968, stocks were hardly a hedge against inflation. On the other hand, to a theoretical investor who bought the 30 Dow Jones Industrials in 1949, when the Average was 160, and who sold them in early 1966, when the average reached approximately 1000, stocks were a great hedge against inflation.

A well-publicized computer study carried out several years ago at the University of Chicago showed that if a theoretical investor made every possible trade on every listed stock every week, beginning in 1926, he would have made an average profit of 9% a year over the more than three decades covered by the computer. This 9% figure comes as close as we can to the average profit you would make each year picking stocks out of a hat and holding them until the end of the year. Inflation over the long term has reduced the purchasing power of the dollar by something closer to 4%. So, it seems that if you are going to adopt a very long term point of view, stocks are more likely than not to serve as an effective hedge against inflation. I should add, however, that the market has almost always been strongest during periods of relative price stability rather than during periods of rapid inflation, such as the 1968–1970 period.

Q. I am enclosing a list of stocks which I picked out of a recent stock guide because they all have price-earnings ratios of less than 9. It would seem to me that these are pretty cheap now and some of them should be good buys. Do you agree?

A. You have picked out an interesting assortment of relatively small and quite speculative companies whose stocks, at recent prices, have been sporting rather low P/E ratios, ranging from five to eight. Looking for low P/Es is a good screening procedure, but you must remember that it is only a first step. The P/E ratios in the stock guide are based on the latest twelve months' earnings. Now you have to do a little detective work to find out if those earnings are going to hold up, improve, or suddenly evaporate. Often when a P/E is very low, it is low because investors are skeptical about the company's *future* earnings, especially for the coming twelve months. Try asking your broker to find you a recent research report on the company. Or you can ask him to call up the company's chief financial officer and find out which way earnings are *headed* and why. But don't believe everything he tells you!

Q. I have recently come into possession of a stock certificate of Bay State Gas Company, issued December 17, 1898. Is it of any value? The American Loan & Trust Company of Boston was registrar of transfers.

A. Call up Standard & Poor's in New York and ask for "central inquiry." Give them the information and they will be able to tell you what happened to the company. The charge is $10. Sometimes a stock in a company that no longer exists turns out to have some value because the company was merged into another company that does still exist.

7

HOW TO REALIZE LONG-TERM GAINS IN TURNAROUND SITUATIONS

One of the authors had the memorable assignment as a financial analyst to investigate Parke, Davis, a company that many doctors used to follow closely. At the time, he was associated on a part-time basis with David J. Greene & Co., which had been following Parke, Davis for many years. The stock had been as high as 50, but had made its way irregularly downward for a period of nine years, and then collapsed completely as everyone gave up on the company.

At the time of the investigation, Parke, Davis was a major drug company that had not introduced a significant new drug in over twenty years, despite millions of dollars spent on research each year. The patent on its biggest seller, the antibiotic, Chloromycetin, had run out, which meant the price of the drug dropped and other manufacturers moved in and began making the drug and selling it still cheaper, while newer antibiotics took over most of Chloromycetin's market (especially after the drug's side effects became widely publicized). Parke, Davis' revenues from the worldwide sale of Chloromycetin had dropped from well over $100 million to about $10 million, and there were no new products to take up the slack. Virtually every major institutional stockholder had eliminated Parke, Davis from its portfolio.

It's All in the Price

The author's trip to Detroit and his investigation of the company confirmed, in every respect, the negative feeling that the investment community had developed over this stock. There was nothing to be seen but antiquated facilities, confusion, a research department that hadn't the vaguest notion of what to do or how to do it, a president who gave out one set of figures while the treasurer gave out another, rising costs, products that were in trouble and losing their markets—in short, a hopeless situation.

At the time the author left for Detroit, the stock had dropped to 18. By the time he got back to the office and began assembling his notes, it had dropped to 15. Before he had a chance to complete his report, the company cut its dividend from $1.00 annually to 50¢.

The boss called him into his office and asked for his impressions of Parke, Davis. He went through a long list of negatives and generally conveyed to him the idea that it was a second-rate company and no one in his right mind would ever buy the stock.

All the while, David J. Greene listened carefully and nodded. The stock was still dropping—was now down to 14, 13⅞, 13¾ . . .

When the oral report was finished, he concluded with the statement that "the picture is full of nothing but negatives, and the company is absolutely a hopeless case."

"I agree with everything you say," said David J. Greene, "but it's all in the price. The price is right." With that pronouncement, the shrewd Wall Street veteran picked up the phone and proceeded to buy the stock. Within a couple of days he had bought for the firm and its clients some 75,000 shares at prices between 13¾ and 14½.

His buying appeared to have formed a bottom in the stock, partly because it was already so thoroughly sold out, and partly because word inevitably got around the street that Greene was buying it. The price, over the next few weeks, edged upward despite the continued negative attitude toward the stock expressed by other drug analysts. Then came the electrifying news that Warner Lambert and Parke, Davis had agreed to merge. Holders of Parke, Davis were to receive over $25 a share in Warner-Lambert stock. The stock responded to the announcement by rising a little further, but there was still widespread skepticism because analysts doubted that the merger would go through. To make a long story short, however, it went through, and Greene and his clients doubled their money.

Moving Against the Mob

What is the moral of this story? The story illustrates some of the most important principles of stock market investing:

(1) One good way to make money in the stock market is to buy a stock when nobody else wants it, and after just about everyone has sold it.

(2) To make money in the stock market, it often helps to ignore the opinions of others and look at the price in relation to the company's underlying assets (including its good name). Greene's comment that "It's all in the price" sums this principle up beautifully. Sure, the company was in terrible shape, but this had long since been discounted in the price of the stock. The price, in fact, had gotten so low that another company in the same industry was able to make an offer substantially above the market and still get itself a bargain.

The price-is-right game can be played by anyone who has developed a good sense of overall market timing. For instance, if you can judge the approximate low point of a bear market, or the approximate bottom of a decline in a group of unpopular stocks during a bull market, or for that matter, the approximate bottom of a decline in a single stock, you can play this highly profitable game without paying any attention to chart patterns and without investigating the company from a fundamental analyst's point of view.

But the important point is that this game requires a strong stomach and a very independent turn of mind. Few people have been able to detach themselves sufficiently from the prevailing sentiment and buy just when everyone is selling furiously in a climactic drop following a long period of weakness. Even when a blue chip company like RCA got down to a bargain-basement 18⅛ in its last real bear market (from a high of 66), most observers were afraid to touch it, fearing it could drop even lower or that it would take years to recover. Six months later, RCA was almost double that bargain-basement price. McGraw-Hill, a publishing giant that had a lot of bad news for its stockholders for many years, got all the way down to 10¼, from a high three years earlier of 57. In less than a year after touching 10¼, it had more than doubled from this low point, *even without any improvement in operations*. At 10¼, in other words, the price was right, despite all the negatives that security analysts were finding out about the company. Yet how many investors were willing to touch it at 10¼, after learning that earnings were still dropping off?

One of the things to aim for in the price-is-right game is the relatively large percentage rebound that can occur in a stock that has gotten down below 10 after a long period of disfavor. If a stock that once sold in the 20's or 30's drops to 6, it may rebound quickly to 9. At 9 it is still way down, from the point of view of someone who bought it at 27. But the person who picked it up at 6 has a 50 percent gain, even though business is terrible and the company is plagued with all kinds of problems.

Obviously, the approach is not as easy as it sounds, and as I have already indicated, some big mistakes have been made by bargain hunters. For example, I know of one highly-regarded investment advisor who decided to buy U.S. Steel at 56 back in early 1962, just after the stock had dropped sharply because of a confrontation between President Kennedy and the steel industry (over price increases). This veteran Wall Streeter figured that U.S. Steel was a bargain at 56, because only a few years earlier it had sold as high as 108. Here, after all, was one of America's largest corporate empires selling more than 50 percent below its recent high, and there had just been a big sell-off resulting from emotional "news" regarding the hassle with the federal government.

The trouble with this investor's tactic was that the industry group in question was still deteriorating badly, and 56 was nowhere near the bottom. A few months later U.S. Steel was in the low 40's, and for the next eight years it continued irregularly downward to 25. By that time the steel industry still hadn't solved its problems, nor had this particular company improved its operations or its outlook. But at 25, compared with a high of 108, the stock was beginning to look as though its problems were "all in the price."

The Earnings Turnaround

If you can foresee a significant earnings turnaround in a company whose earnings have been declining and whose stock has been dropping because of the poor earnings, you may have a situation that could produce very substantial capital gains. This is especially true if you can time your purchase correctly, when the price is right. When a company's earnings are about to deteriorate, many stockholders have already sold, and the price has already eroded. When the lower earnings finally show up, there is often more selling, especially if the earnings downtrend continues for more than a year. In other words, the bandwagon effect described earlier comes into play, and the decline in the stock becomes overdone. The subsequent recovery is also likely to be overdone, especially if earnings really do turn around. The object, in turnaround situations, is to time your trades in order to take advantage of the *exaggerated swings* that are so characteristic of the stock market, both on the way down and on the way up.

When you get right down to it, all you have to do to find a real earnings turnaround situation is a little homework. You don't have to be a financial wizard. You just have to be willing to take the trouble to find out the facts. It is amazing how few people do bother to find things out on Wall Street. Most of them would rather accept a vague rumor than check it out, even though checking it out is often relatively simple.

Taking Advantage of a "Special Situation"

A stock qualifies as a special situation if some specific corporate action, such as a merger, acquisition, spinoff, or major change of business, is imminent and is likely to make the stock go up. Usually the special situation hunter is on the lookout for a takeover candidate—a company that stands a good chance of being acquired in the near future at a price substantially higher than the current market. That, in fact, is a guessing game in itself and will be discussed in the next chapter. Let's look at another type of special situation, in which many specific corporate actions were involved.

The Example of Swift & Co.

Most people recognize the name Swift as the nation's largest meat packer. It also happens to be one of the thirty stocks included in the Dow Jones Industrial Average. For many years this stock fluctuated widely, with relatively little net upward progress. The company's profit margins were thin, so that changes in the fortunes of the meat packing business, from year to year, had sizable effects on earnings per share. Investors tended to regard the stock as strictly cyclical rather than as a growth situation, and as a result the price-earnings ratio remained below average.

An ambitious new management got control of Swift and began making drastic plans for improved profitability. Briefly, their aim was to get rid of all of Swift's marginal and least profitable facilities, and to use the money from the sale of these assets for more profitable businesses—enterprises with higher profit margins. The plan sounded simple enough and obvious enough. After all, if you can sell a business whose profit is relatively small and put the money into one whose profit is much bigger, you should come out way ahead.

But it was only the analysts who did their homework and really looked into the company who realized the dimensions of the potential improvement. Some $200,000,000 of facilities were to be sold. Moreover, if the money could be put to good use, it was not unreasonable to predict that this company, which had been averaging about $1.50

a share of earnings, could eventually earn about $4.00 a share. If so, the stock could, at the least, be expected to double as the company's massive realignment plans materialized.

As this chapter went to press, Swift had just about completed its redeployment of assets, and earnings were on their way to the projected figure of $4.00 (although they hadn't reached that figure yet). What was formerly a meat packing company was now also an oil company, to say nothing of its large interests in insurance, chemicals, foods, and other businesses. The important point is that the new businesses are far more profitable than those the company disposed of. Investors who studied the company after hearing of the redeployment plans had ample opportunity to buy the stock before it began rising in response to the higher earnings. The redeployment process took a number of years, but it was a classical example of the special situation investment.

How to Avoid Just Fumbling Around

It is surprising how many investors keep making the same mistake over and over again. They may buy near a top every time, or get scared into selling near the bottom of a panic every time, or they may continually buy on hunches, or take their profits much too soon, or plunge into the market all at once and sell out all at once. And so on. In so many cases, the individual investor seems to have his own characteristic behavior pattern which leads him to make his own characteristic mistakes again and again. And many of those who do not follow such a set pattern tend to just fumble around—buying a stock, getting annoyed because it doesn't go up right away, and selling (only to watch it go up afterward), then buying another one, which doesn't move for six months, selling it, and so it goes—a lot of sound and fury with no profit. Many advisory services, as well as individual investors, fumble around in just this way.

Somehow or other, the idea of learning from experience escapes most people when it comes to investing. Yet, if one doesn't learn from experience, the experience is wasted.

The investor should begin with certain definite criteria for stock selection and he should be very clear on his investment objective. For example, he may decide that he wants to confine his selections to one of the categories described in this chapter, and that his objective is to hold the stock for eighteen months or thereabouts, and to sell half of the investment at that time, on the assumption that it will have risen 40 percent to 50 percent by then. Part of the plan would also be to hold the remaining half for another eighteen months, just in case the selection was very good and the stock continues to appreciate.

Every few months, moreover, he should go back over his investment decisions and notice exactly what went wrong or what proved right, and why it did. On the basis of these periodic reviews, he may decide to revise his principles and objectives. But even so, he should stick to the revised guidelines and review *them* periodically too, so that they can be improved on the basis of experience.

Because of the excitement and tension often created by a fluctuating stock market, emotional distractions usually lead to hasty and ill-advised buy and sell decisions. The biggest problem is how to avoid being influenced by the emotional distractions. This is best handled by having a definite set of principles and objectives and sticking to them until experience indicates that they should be modified.

Our favorite "system" is to sell half of a stock after it doubles, and a fourth after it doubles again. That way, you get your money back and still keep the original amount invested in the same stock. Of course, in order to use this system, you have to have enough luck and/or skill to have chosen a stock that goes up a long way. But it is a good example of an investment objective that you set forth ahead of time and stick to. It takes the emotions and the guesswork out of deciding when to sell.

In most cases, another set of criteria will be needed in determining when to sell. One old professional suggests this arrangement: Any stock should be considered a sell candidate, subject to further investigation, of course, if its price drops by a specified amount that you have decided upon ahead of time. This guideline should protect the investor against heavy losses resulting from an unexpectedly prolonged decline. He uses the *square root principal:* If a $100 stock drops 10 points, or if a $49 stock drops 7 points, or a $9 stock drops 3 points, etc., it should be sold, or at least be quickly investigated, on the assumption that something may be radically wrong with the company. Sometimes, with a little investigation you can find out exactly what is wrong, but often the overt signs of trouble may only appear later on. Market action tends to anticipate both trouble and progress.

This, of course, would not apply during a severe market decline, when most stocks might be dropping by their square roots. It is applicable during a bull market, or a sideward market, and is something like a stop-loss order, which some traders consider a kind of insurance policy against heavy losses.

QUESTIONS AND ANSWERS

Q. I would appreciate your explanation of the term, so commonly used, "leverage."

A. A stock is sometimes said to be leveraged when a slight pickup in business means a big jump in earnings. This would be true of a company with high fixed costs, such as a relatively heavy debt in relation to the amount of common stock.

Q. If a stock's dividend has recently been cut or omitted, is that a logical stock to avoid?

A. It may be logical to avoid it, but the market is seldom logical. As a matter of fact, one recent study of the performance of stocks after dividend omissions showed that these stocks outperformed the market averages two or three times over during the ensuing year.

The most likely explanation of this phenomenon is that stocks go down in anticipation of a dividend omission, and once the omission is actually announced, the worst is over and the stocks start back up again. Usually, when stocks go down, they go down too far, and when they go up, they go up too far.

8

HOW INDICATORS CAN HELP
AN INVESTOR'S TIMING

Making money in the stock market is as much a matter of timing as picking the right stocks. When the bear romp starts, you can have the best stock on the list—it's still not going to go up. Conversely, when every barber and taxi driver is buying and the whole list is climbing, it's hard not to win. The real art is in knowing when to jump into the market and, more importantly, when to tuck your tail between your legs and run.

There are all kinds of indicators to help you time the swings in the market, some of them based on sound economic principles, others on superstition. There probably are as many market players who depend on astrologers to tell them what to do as there are people who follow the statistics of money supply and bond-to-stock yield ratios. While we don't deny that the stars may control destinies at the corner of Broad and Wall as well as anywhere else, we confess to having no particular expertise in the occult arts and so will confine ourselves to noting some of the more mundane auguries. We will also confess that they are far from infallible.

Consult the Indexes

One of the easiest roadsigns to follow is the Department of Commerce index of leading economic indicators, which is readily available in that agency's monthly publication, *Business Conditions Digest,* which you can get from the Government Printing Office in Washington for $15 a year. Its object, to be sure, is not to forecast stock prices, but to help businessmen keep track of the ups and downs of the business cycle. Since the latter is one of the primary influences on the course of stock prices, however, it amounts to the same thing.

The Commerce Department takes all its statistical series, like carloadings, unemployment, building permits, etc., and checks them historically to see whether they are leading, coincident or lagging—that is, whether they move concurrently with the business cycle, ahead of it, or behind. Then it works up an index for each one. Naturally, the one we're interested in is the index of leading indicators, since it is the one that has forecasting potential—experience shows that it moves about six months in advance of any turn in the business cycle.

Trouble is, so does the stock market. In fact, right at the top of the list of components in the leading indicator index is stock prices. Consequently, it would seem likely that a stock market trader who depends on the index to call the turns for him is likely to get his signals a little late. Particularly in anticipating bear markets, which pick up momentum like a run on the bank, it would seem to be useless. However, that is not entirely the case, since some of the other components are very quick on the draw. They include prices of industrial materials, new factory orders for durable goods, the average work week, building permits, new orders for plant and equipment, new claims for unemployment insurance, and the ratio of prices to unit labor costs.

The average business cycle is 52 months long, from peak to peak. The periods of expansion normally last 33 months and the recessions 19 months. The sharpest rise in stocks usually occurs in the final months of a recession and the early months of a recovery; then the bull market usually just peters out gradually and turns to bear. On the downside, by way of contrast, the sharpest declines usually precede the turn, carrying out the old adage that it's always darkest just before the dawn.

Dow Theory Signals Not Reliable

One of the most widely followed systems for forecasting the stock market is the Dow Theory, which corresponds to the technical approach in picking individual stocks. It's based on the proposition that the stock market is its own best oracle, tracing patterns on the charts which, if only you know how to read them, will give you the tip-off on what's going to happen.

Elaborated by Clarence Dow, one of the editors of the *Wall Street Journal,* early in the century, the Dow Theory was further refined by his successors in that post. Now, however, its high priest is an analyst named Richard Russell who puts out a market letter called *Dow Theory Letters.* The Dow-Jones publications, *Wall Street Journal* and *Barron's,* seldom refer to it, except somewhat slightingly when market developments indicate that buying or selling by followers of the theory are having an effect on the market.

A number of books have been written on the Dow Theory, and, to be frank, a good-sized tome is required to explain it adequately. What seems to happen is that every time the market fails to perform as forecast, which occurs frequently, the theory is refined further to account for the aberration. In essence, though, it holds that the trend of the market will continue in whatever direction it is going until something happens to make it change direction; meanwhile, it will proceed hesitantly, two steps forward and one back, three steps forward and two back, etc., but always irregularly. The time to watch out is when a major peak doesn't go as high as the preceding one, on the upside, or in a bear market, when a valley doesn't cut as deep as the one before it. Such a formation is likely to signal a turn, but only if it is "confirmed" by a similar action of the

Dow-Jones Transportation Average. (The primary one to watch, of course, is the Industrial Average, made up of thirty blue chip stocks.)

Frequently, it's easier to explain market action in terms of the Dow Theory by means of hindsight, six months after a turn takes place, than when it's happening. Nevertheless, one should not discount it entirely. Because so many market players follow it, the Dow Theory comes close to being a self-fulfilling prognosticator. Especially in the late stages of a bull market, any time the charts show a squiggle that might be taken as a bear signal, a wave of selling will depress the market, at least temporarily.

Odd-Lotters Sometimes Tip the Market's Hand

One of the most disconcerting systems of market analysis, for those of us who admit to being small investors, is the Odd Lot Survey. It is based on the thesis that, collectively, small investors tend to be wrong when the market reaches a turning point and starts a new trend. If you go into the market at a time when most of the little people are getting out, and vice-versa, you'll make out fine. How do you know what the masses of small investors are doing? Easy. Just chart the trend of odd-lot (less than 100 share) transactions reported every day by Carlisle DeCoppet & Co. on the financial pages. Investors who buy odd lots are assumed to be financially unable to buy round (100 shares or more) lots and are therefore not only small, but also foolish.

The idea of predicating a whole market theory on the fallibility of the odd-lotter is attributed to an analyst named Garfield Drew, who, for years, sold a market letter charting odd-lot activity. Like the Dow Theory, however, Drew's system had to be refined every time it turned out to be mistaken, and lately an economics professor named Martin Zweig has discovered a new and improved patsy, the odd-lot short seller. Mr. Zweig, who also sells a market letter, cites statistics going back nearly thirty years to show that people who sell short in odd lots are consistently wrong.

Of course there's always a first time for everything, and it would be just like those stupid odd-lot short sellers to be right when you're betting against them.

Watch the Money Supply

Roger Williams, former chief economist at Standard & Poor's, the largest investment advisory service, spends most of his working days trying to forecast general business conditions and trends in the economy. Scholarly, thorough, and extremely cautious, he never makes a forecast until he has a veritable mountain of relevant facts marshalled behind it. Then, when he finally predicts, he does so with conviction.

According to Mr. Williams, the main thing you need to know at any given time, in order to evaluate the strength of the economy for the immediate future, is the rate of change in the money supply, which is defined as the total amount of currency in circulation, plus the sum of all the nation's checking accounts. A rapidly expanding money supply tends to stimulate business and fuel inflation, whereas a money supply that is contracting, holding even, or expanding too slowly tends to dampen business and act as a brake on inflation. Figures on the money supply, bank credit and other monetary aggregates are reported in the *Wall Street Journal* and the *New York Times* every Friday and *Barron's* each week. Continuing analysis of what the figures mean can be found in the *Survey of Current Business,* published by the Federal Reserve Bank of New York.

Control over the money supply is exercised primarily by the Federal Reserve through its Open Market Committee, which meets every month, reviews the state of the U.S. economy, and decides whether to loosen or tighten the purse strings. Its decisions are made public only a month or so later, after they have already been put into effect and it's too late for market speculators to act on the information. If it is determined that the money supply needs to be expanded, the committee quietly starts buying government securities, particularly Treasury bills, on the open market (hence the committee's name). And where does it get the money to buy the securities? No problem. It has it printed at the mint. Naturally, when this new money gets into circulation, via the bank accounts of securities dealers, it tends to puff up the economy. Suddenly, there's more money chasing the same goods and services; prices go up and demand strengthens. To slow things down, the committee sells government securities on the open market, thus taking money out of circulation.

The "Fed" has other means of influencing the course of the economy besides the activities of the open market committee. It controls the size of reserves which member banks must hold, and by minor changes in its rules it is thus able to expand or contract the amount of money they have available for loans. If it wants to slow down the economy, it can also close its rediscount window, where banks borrow against commercial paper when they are strapped for funds, or it can raise the rediscount interest rate, forcing the banks to hike their rates. How effective the "Fed" can be was amply illustrated in late 1969 and early 1970 when, in its efforts to halt inflation, the "Fed" forced interest rates to historic highs and created a money crunch that brought the economy to its knees. The stock market, of course, went into a tailspin.

The 1969–70 recession and the recovery in 1971–72 was a hard lesson for stock market players, who thereby learned to keep a sharp eye peeled for changes in Federal Reserve policy. It is not likely, however, that the experience will be repeated any time soon, since it wasn't very successful and, presumably, the "Fed" also learned a lesson. It slammed on the brakes so hard in 1969 that the economic distress became intolerable, yet the rate of inflation was not slowed appreciably. Certainly, if the "Fed" had continued to hold the economy in a financial straightjacket, it eventually would have brought about a condition of disinflation, but that was politically impossible. Then, when it shifted its stance and began pumping money into the economic bloodstream again, it rediscovered an old axiom: pushing on a purse string is not as effective as pulling it. Long months and inordinate amounts of paper money were required to get business moving again. Meanwhile, wage-price controls had to be instituted to keep inflation from getting completely out of hand.

Still, the money supply and Federal Reserve policy will continue to have a profound effect on the stock market, and anyone who has money in the market should be constantly on the alert for any shifts in direction. Investors should also keep an eye out for factors that are likely to influence "Fed" policy. One, of course, is inflation, as reflected in the wholesale price index. Any sustained rise is very likely to lead to money-tightening moves by the "Fed." Conversely, when unemployment creeps up, the open market committee is almost bound to start buying government securities. Those two, the wholesale price index and the rate of unemployment, are the Scylla and Charybdis between which the "Fed" steers a precarious course.

The other element constantly tugging on the "Fed's" sleeve is the flow of money in international trade. When President Nixon notified the world, on August 15, 1971, that the U.S. no longer would pay its obligations in gold and subsequently devalued the dollar, he dealt a death blow to the Bretton Woods agreement which, since World War II, had formed the basis for an international monetary system. At the time this was written, it had been replaced only by makeshift agreements hammered out at the Smithsonian conference and at meetings of the Bank for International Settlements in Basle, Switzerland. The principal goal of these agreements was to prevent great tidal waves of "hot money" from flowing into one country or another and overwhelming its monetary system. To help keep the system on an even keel, the "Fed" is obligated to maintain the value of the dollar, as far as possible, and to avoid creating any imbalance in interest rates which would cause such a tidal wave. Early in 1972, when declining interest rates in the U.S. once more set up a hot-money flow into West Germany and France, the "Fed" hastened to correct the situation. Also importantly influencing the "Fed" are the borrowing requirements of the Treasury; when the latter is about to float a big issue of bonds or bills, the "Fed" acts to hold money markets steady.

What Stocks to Buy When Interest Rates Are Changing

Roger Williams has made up a list of stock groups that tend to exhibit market strength when interest rates are falling, and another for periods of rising rates. The former are called "interest sensitive" and the latter "cycle sensitive." When the market is healthy but interest rates are moving up, buy the cycle-sensitive stocks. When the market is healthy but interest rates are falling, turn to the interest-sensitive group. When the market is not healthy, get into a cash position no matter which way interest rates are going. The groups are listed in approximate order of their sensitivity to interest rate trends.

Interest Sensitive

Utilities, high-grade common stocks, building, finance, small loans, natural gas distributors, fire and casualty insurance, confectionery, biscuit bakers, food chains, soap, banks, food processors, cement, chemicals, bread and cake bakers, corn refiners, dairy products, packaged foods, machinery, vegetable oils, natural gas pipelines, telephone companies, life insurance.

Cycle Sensitive

Automobiles, trucks, construction machinery, railroads, electric appliances, machine tools, agricultural machinery, miscellaneous metals, synthetic fibers, tire and rubber, capital goods, low-priced common stocks, aluminum, heating and plumbing, copper, home furnishings, lead and zinc, industrial machinery, metal fabricators, broadcasters, radio and TV, steel, textiles, airlines, paper, railroad equipment.

QUESTIONS AND ANSWERS

Q. I have noticed over the years that whenever a bull market approaches its peak, my patients are loaded with hot tips on the stock market. I wonder if I have discovered a new indicator that all doctors can use. Should I write a book about it?

A. What you have discovered is really one of the oldest and most tried and tested indicators around: the contrary opinion indicator (see Chapter 18). When everybody and his uncle thinks that stocks are going up, stocks have already gone up and will probably go down.

Q. The odd lot figures show that the public has been selling more than buying. Isn't this a bullish sign?

A. Not necessarily. But if they increase their selling in relation to buying over the coming weeks, that would probably be a bullish omen. The important thing is the *trend* of odd-lot buying and selling over a period of time, not just the absolute figures for one period of time.

Q. Have there been any statistical studies showing that stocks tend to be stronger at certain times of the year and weaker at other times?·

A. There have been statistical studies correlating the stock market's fluctuations with the constellations in the sky, with the density of electromagnetic waves in the air, with the length of women's skirts, and with almost anything else you might care to mention. As to seasonal influences, the market usually rallies in late December and early January, but other than that, I don't think there is any point to such correlations.

9

HOW TO READ A FINANCIAL STATEMENT WITH A "PROFESSIONAL" EYE

Some professional men tend to shy away from stock market investments because, not being accountants or even businessmen, they feel lost when confronted with the fundamental tool of the investor, the company financial statement. Overcoming a lack of know-how in that area, moreover, looks like a formidable task—at best, wading through a long, boring book on accounting. Well, the fact is that it's not all that difficult. To be sure, reading one brief chapter here isn't going to make an accountant out of you, but most investment decisions aren't made in accordance with accounting principles anyway. If they were, CPAs wouldn't be scribbling in ledgers for a living.

What We Look For Today

Time was when the first thing you wanted to know about an investment was the yield—the dividend (or coupon payment in the case of a bond) divided by the price. The second thing was how well the yield was protected—in other words, how soundly financed the company was and, therefore, how likely it would be to continue its regular payout. Anyone with a little financial acumen could figure those things out by glancing at the annual statement. The income tax and the preferential rate for capital gains, however, changed all that. Today, only insurance companies and executors of trust funds are interested in bonds, and they are getting over it. Common stocks with a high payout. Anyone with a little financial acumen could figure those things out by glancing minded. What we're interested in today is *capital appreciation*—the price of the stock should go up—and we know that what will make it happen is earnings growth. That old earnings-per-share figure has got to keep climbing. Whether it will do so usually has less to do with the figures you're going to read in the annual statement than with the products the company makes, how tough its competition is, and how lively are the slogans its advertising agency dreams up.

Nevertheless, being able to read the firm's financial statement may protect us from some unpleasant surprises. Many a hot stock that suddenly cooled did so because a savvy analyst took a look at the figures and blew the whistle.

For purpose of illustration, let's take a specific example, the annual statement of a small motor boat manufacturer called Uniflite, Inc., chosen simply because it is uncomplicated:

Balance Sheet

ASSETS	1970	1969
Current Assets:		
Cash	$ 119,139	$ 140,827
Receivables	1,323,464	1,224,128
Less provision for doubtful accounts	(55,000)	(55,100)
Costs in excess of billings on uncompleted		
U.S. Government contracts	2,089	283,517
Inventories, at lower of cost or market		
Completed boats	413,980	366,310
Work in process	143,251	181,399
Raw materials and supplies	801,162	582,156
Prepaid expenses	13,131	33,197
Total current assets	$2,761,216	$2,756,434
Plant and equipment, at cost:		
Leasehold improvements:		
Buildings	483,343	483,561
Other facilities	288,121	276,912
Machinery, equipment and furniture	338,381	319,355
Allowances for depreciation and amortization	(423,342)	(340,874)
	$ 686,503	$ 738,954
Unamortized patterns, molds and plugs	130,833	109,616
Deferred federal income taxes	15,000	19,000
	$3,618,419	$3,653,263
LIABILITIES		
Current liabilities:		
Note payable to bank	$ 150,000	$ 350,000
Current portion of long-term debt	53,200	52,900
Accounts payable, trade	1,065,969	912,927
Federal income taxes:		
Currently payable	126,704	—
Deferred credit	29,000	154,000
Other accrued and withheld taxes	67,169	68,359
Other accrued expenses	38,122	58,921
Total current liabilities	$1,530,164	$1,597,107
Long-term debt, net of current portion	19,388	72,476
	$1,549,552	$1,669,583

STOCKHOLDERS' EQUITY

Common stock, par $.66⅔, authorized
    1,500,000 shares, issued and out-

standing 504,900 shares	336,599	336,599
Capital in excess of par value	696,481	696,481
Retained earnings	1,035,787	950,600
Total stockholders' equity	$2,068,867	$1,983,680
	$3,618,419	$3,653,263

Statement of Income and Retained Earnings

Income	1970	1969
Net sales	$6,825,991	$7,804,248
Costs and expenses:		
Cost of products sold	5,781,521	6,931,808
Selling, general and administrative expenses	810,755	740,217
Interest	48,528	28,580
Income (pre-tax)	$ 185,187	$ 103,643
Federal income taxes		
Current	209,000	233,000
Deferred	121,000	183,000
	$ 97,187	$ 53,643
Cost of litigation settlement	12,000	—
Net income	$ 85,187	$ 53,643
Net income per share	.17	.11
Retained earnings, beginning of year	$950,600	1,102,382
Deduct dividends:		
Cash, $.05	—	24,750
Stock, 2%	—	180,675
Retained earnings, end of year	$1,035,787	$ 950,600

A Curious Situation

The first thing to look at is the income statement, or profit and loss sheet. Here, we note immediately that sales in 1970 declined from their 1969 level, which was not unusual in 1970, a down year for the U.S. economy in general. What is interesting is that Uniflite was able to increase its profits significantly during the year, despite lower volume. We note, also, that the improvement was due to cost-cutting in the product area, not in "selling, general and administrative expenses," which went up. Mental note: did quality decline? Another mental note: interest cost rose sharply, although a quick glance at the balance sheet shows that debt, both long-term and the bank note, was cut 'way down. Thumbing quickly through the written report, we find an explanation:

During 1970, Uniflite worked out a deal with a finance company "to provide a national program for Uniflite dealer financing." Moving on, we find a curious situation: income taxes for both 1969 and 1970 were more than net income; had not a portion of taxes been deferred in both years, the company would have operated in the red. The notes provide an explanation: Uniflite makes boats for both the consumer market and the U.S. Navy; "Deferred federal income taxes arise principally from differences in the financial statement and tax treatment of retainages on U.S. Government contracts." Doesn't make much sense, but let's move along.

Net income, we discover, was only 1.3 percent of sales in 1969 and 1.6 percent in 1970. The company's profit margin, obviously, is paper-thin. Then we discover that, although profits took a 50 percent jump, the firm found it prudent to eliminate in 1970 the cash and stock dividends it declared in 1969. At the time, Uniflite shares were selling in the over-the-counter market at 4¾ bid. On earnings of 17 cents per share, we figure out a price-earnings ratio of 28:1—extremely high for a small company which has just cut its dividend. AT&T then was selling at only eleven times earnings.

Information on the Balance Sheet

Turning to the balance sheet, the first thing to look at is the company's working capital position—current assets less current liabilities. In this case, assets exceed liabilities $2.7 million to $1.5 million for a current ratio of 1.7 to 1. Normally, this is the most important figure to be gleaned from the balance sheet. For a small company in a highly volatile business, Uniflite's current ratio is quite thin; for safety, it should be at least 2 to 1.

A related area in which Uniflite looks weak is in its ratio of quick assets to current liabilities. Quick assets are those that can be quickly turned into cash, normally current ones minus inventories, and for a manufacturing company they should exceed current liabilities by a comfortable margin. Uniflite's current liabilities, however, exceed its quick assets by over $150,000.

Take a look at Uniflite's inventory position. It has over half a million dollars in finished products and work in process. That's only 20 percent of current assets, which isn't excessive, and amounts to only about 10 percent of annual sales. However, with sales declining, inventories of raw materials jumped 37 percent year-to-year—not good. Uniflite has no bonded indebtedness, but if it did we would have to look at the "coverage." To do that, you subtract intangible assets (such as goodwill, patents, etc.) and current liabilities from total assets, which gives the amount theoretically available to pay off the bondholders in case of liquidation.

An oft-cited figure, to be determined by examination of the balance sheet, is book value, or the amount of money each stockholder presumably would receive if the company were to be liquidated. It is determined by adding up the stockholders' equity items, in this case common stock, capital in excess of par value and retained earnings, and dividing by the number of shares outstanding—504,900. In this case, it comes out to $4.09 per share, not much less than the quoted price for the stock—$4.75. For a company in a supposedly growth industry like boating to be selling so close to book is unusual. It's either a bargain, or something is wrong with the firm. To be sure, 1970 was a year when stocks of many companies were selling close to book value, and if they survived they were, in truth, bargains.

More significant than book value, as a rule, is the degree of leverage exerted by the company, which is determined by comparing the amount of bonds and preferred stock with the common stock outstanding. Uniflite, it will be noted, has issued neither bonds nor preferred, so we say that the company is not leveraged, but some firms, especially the conglomerates, which made their appearance in such numbers in the latter 1960's, frequently were leveraged in a ratio of 10 to 1. A high degree of leverage raises the profit potential of a company in good times, but also increases the risk that it may go broke in hard times. That is why, in the 1969–71 recession, Wall Street sold off the stocks of conglomerates so heavily. Since a number of them did plunge into bankruptcy and the earnings of others plummeted, the Street for once was right.

Not to keep the reader any longer in suspense about Uniflite, let's see how accurate our analysis was. On the plus side, earnings were up, despite a drop in sales volume, and on the basis of book vs. quoted value the stock looked like a bargain. On the other hand, inventories of raw materials looked excessive and the company's financial condition was nothing to boast about—it lacked liquidity. Probably most important, the company was changing its marketing emphasis from being defense-oriented—making tenders for the Navy—to fishing boats and other pleasure craft. In the process it was taking a serious gamble—financing dealer inventories. Anyone familiar with the parlous state of the motorboat market in 1970 would have thought three times before buying Uniflite stock.

So what happened? In 1971 the company's sales jumped to $7.6 million, and earnings more than doubled, to 38 cents per share. The price of the shares soared from 4¾ to 13½. All of which bears out what we were saying at the start—financial analysis has its place, but what you really need to know about a company—quality of its products, strength of its management and marketing organization, competition—are not always to be found in its financial statements.

But we still haven't looked at the most important part of any financial statement, the notes. You need good eyes for this, because the notes are always in fine print, tucked away in the back of the annual report. They contain the information which the Securities and Exchange Commission requires the company to tell about itself, but which it isn't particularly anxious to bring to stockholder attention. Veteran security analysts, after a quick glance at the upward or downward trend of earnings-per-share, usually turn immediately to the notes.

What the Notes Reveal

What you're looking for is the devious, the contrived little formulation that explains but doesn't explain, the hook. It takes a bit of practice, but after a while you become adept at sniffing out little artifices and deceptions which throw up red flags about investing in the company's stock. One of the best places to find them is in the paragraph that tells how certain costs have been capitalized—to be amortized over a period of years, rather than expensed during the current year. This was a favorite device of the computer service companies, so many of which went broke during the 1969–71 recession. At the start, they capitalized the cost of developing computer programs they hoped to sell, which was perfectly legitimate. But after a time, it got to the point where they simply decided how much earnings they wanted to show in a particular year, in order to attract investors; then, they made the figure on the bottom line come out as desired by capitalizing as many costs as necessary.

Another nifty device is the pooling-of-interests trick, which the conglomerates developed into a fine art in the late 1960s. The idea is that, when two companies merge, the earnings of the combination are shown as though they had "pooled their interests" some time ago. All very well, but suppose the conglomerate has taken over a big retailing chain as of November 30th. Earnings for the year are reported as if they had married at the start of the fourth quarter—the big Christmas selling season for the retailer. The conglomerate's earnings thus soar upward, boosting the stock quotation, and nothing is said about the retail chain's losses for the first three quarters of the year.

Our all-time favorite footnote was the one which explained that the president had sold off practically all of his holdings in the company "in order to augment the liquidity of stockholders' shares."

Finally, always give a quick glance at the auditors' report. Usually it's a set formula: "We have examined the balance sheet of XYZ Co. as of December 31, 1972 and the related statements of income and retained earnings . . ." After reading a few, you can recite it from memory. But every once in a while there's an exception. The auditors, it seems, have a few reservations about whether the financial statements "present fairly the financial position . . . in conformity with generally accepted accounting principles applied on a consistent basis."

Then, watch out.

QUESTIONS AND ANSWERS

Q. What is the meaning of the term "cash flow," and how important is it?

A. Cash flow is earnings plus depreciation. The higher the amount of depreciation in relation to net income, the more important the cash flow per share figure is in determining a stock's worth. If a stock sells at 20 times earnings but only 7 times cash flow per share, it is cheaper than another stock in the same industry selling at 17 times earnings and 12 times cash flow (all other things being more or less equal).

Q. Would you please comment on the relative merit of a company with no debt or preferred stock, compared to one that has long-term debt or preferred stock ahead of the common stock?

A. A company with nothing ahead of the common stock is a more conservative investment (all other things being equal). However, if we are speaking about an industry that is ready for a turnaround in its fortunes, the stock with a lot of debt or preferred ahead of it may be much more leveraged, and therefore the turnaround could be much more spectacular and the percentage gain or loss much greater. It is a case of "the further out on the dog's tail, the wider the swing."

10

WHEN UTILITIES ARE GOOD BUYS FOR THE PROFESSIONAL MAN

Most individual investors seeking capital gains overlook the utility stocks. They think of these stocks as being more like bonds, offering good yields but moving rather slowly if at all. This widespread impression, however, ignores the fact that the electric utility industry has never stopped growing, and that there is hardly any other industry in which future growth is so assured.

The Edison Electric Institute tells us that by 1980 investor-owned utilities expect to have almost double the electric power-producing capacity they had in 1970, and 3½ times that of 1960. Moreover, the total investment in electric power plants, which was $92 billion in 1970, is expected to reach $175 billion by 1975, as the average annual use of electricity in the home continues to rise, and the number of homes rises too.

Looking at the Institute's combined income statement for all investor-owned electric utilities, we find that net income after taxes was 3.13 billion in 1969; 2.96 billion in 1968; 2.88 billion in 1967; 2.72 billion in 1966; 2.56 billion in 1965; 2.36 billion in 1964; 2.17 billion in 1963; and 2.08 billion in 1962. That is not only growth, but steady, uninterrupted growth. And the pattern is expected to continue.

Despite the impressive growth record and the obvious reasons for anticipating further growth, the utility stocks are not always sure bets. You have to buy them at the right time, and at the right price.

Interest Rates and Utility Stock Prices

During the bull market of the 1950s and 1960s, the utility stocks reached their peak prices in 1965, several years before most other stocks did. Between 1965 and 1970, as interest rates throughout the economy rose sharply, utility stock prices fell off steadily, as did the prices of bonds and other fixed-income securities. Price-earnings ratios for utilities declined from their 1965 levels of 18–20 down to 11–12 times earnings by mid-1970. The main reason for the loss of favor was the rise in interest rates. Utilities are big borrowers. They are constantly floating new bonds, new issues of preferred stock, or new common stock, to finance their expansion programs. Typically, a utility's financing is about 54 percent bonds or other long-term debt, 10 percent preferred stock, and 36 percent common stock (based on the Edison Electric Institute's figures).

When interest rates rise, the cost of borrowing goes up, and for the electric utility companies, interest costs are the largest single cost item (not counting taxes). Thus, with costs rising, profits are squeezed—but only temporarily.

The Fair Rate of Return

What saves the utilities from a continual squeeze on profits, and what makes the utility stocks a sound hedge against long-term inflation, is the "fair rate of return" concept that is built into the regulation of electric power companies. These companies are monopolies that are regulated by the state, and the state regulatory authorities fix the rates the companies charge for electric power. Under the protection provided by the Constitution, the states must allow the utilities to earn a fair rate of return on their investment in the production and distribution of electric power. Just what constitutes a fair return varies somewhat from one state to another. But in recent years, the regulatory authorities have allowed the utilities to earn 7 percent or more on invested capital. When the companies do better than this they are usually asked to lower the rates they charge for electric power. When the results fall below this normal, the companies usually ask for permission to raise rates, and usually after extensive hearings, at which the public is represented and raises strong objections, a substantial part of the increase requested is granted.

The state regulatory authorities must see to it that utility stocks and bonds remain attractive to investors, because the electric utilities must continually expand their capacity to meet the rising demand for electricity. To finance this expansion, they must continually sell more bonds and more stock. And to be able to do this, the stocks and bonds must compete with other stocks and bonds. Therefore, the states must grant the utilities adequate rate increases, when needed, in order to make sure that the utility stocks will be attractive to investors. In this respect, the electric utility industry has a virtually built-in guarantee of rising profits, and utility stocks are the surest growth stocks there are, over the long run.

Two Approaches to Capital Gains in the Utilities

In areas of the country that are growing rapidly, the electric power companies enjoy rapidly rising sales. Their operations become more profitable by themselves. Often, in such cases, the state agencies have ordered the companies to cut their rates to customers. But even with the reduction in charges, earnings per share have continued to rise.

In areas where the consumption of electricity is increasing only slightly, the power companies' costs may be rising faster than revenues. Profitability decreases, and the company applies for a rate increase. When granted, the rate increase not only restores the fair rate of return, but enables the company to resume its long-term pattern of rising earnings per share. Moreover, demand for electricity is so compelling that, unlike other industries, in the utility industry an increase in rates has never resulted in a decrease in consumption.

There are, therefore, two approaches to buying utility stocks for capital gains. One is to buy a utility where rapid growth in electric power sales is likely over the coming years. The other is to buy one that will shortly receive the benefits of a rate increase. In either case, earnings per share may be expected to rise. But here is the trick that many investors miss: The rapid growth utilities are usually selling at much higher price-earnings multiples than the slower-growth utilities. *It is often possible to buy one of the latter stocks at a very cheap P/E ratio, before a rate increase materializes. After the rate increase is granted, earnings rise significantly, and the earnings multiple may improve too, resulting in worthwhile capital gains.* In other words, by buying the right utility at the right time, the investor can take advantage of certain cyclical factors that are peculiar to this industry, and achieve capital gains in what is basically a somewhat staid sector of the stock market. And the risk in such transactions is relatively low. Let's look at this same idea from another angle.

Inflation and the Utilities

During periods of rapid inflation and sharply rising interest rates, the typical investor will shy away from utilities for two reasons. First, because he thinks of them almost as fixed-income securities (which they certainly are *not,* as evidenced by the continual increase in dividend rates, even in periods of declining markets) and fears they will go down in price along with the bond market. Second, because he knows that the cost of borrowing new money, either to refinance old bonds that are maturing or to float new ones, will increase as interest rates generally increase. Also, he knows that other costs, such as fuel, equipment, and labor will rise, while any offsetting rise in revenues must await permission to raise rates. As a result, there is apt to be heavy selling of utility stocks by institutions wishing to switch into stocks with more obvious inflation-hedging characteristics, or into more speculative stocks that would go up during an inflationary boom.

If this persists and utility stocks go substantially lower, as they did, for instance, in the late 1960's, the investor should sit up and take notice. Some excellent recovery opportunities may be materializing, as well as some very high yields. Since many investors are wary of the time lag between rising costs and rate relief, all you have to do is be willing to wait a little longer than most people, maybe only a few months longer, to reap the combined benefit of a high yield and significant capital gain.

It should also be noted that while coal is a major cost item, most utilities have clauses in their rate schedules permitting them to pass on much or all of any increase in coal costs to the customers—sometimes just the industrial customers, sometimes to all customers.

Which Ones to Buy

The following is a list of the largest utility operating companies and the largest holding companies (which own operating companies in one integrated area).

Baltimore Gas & Electric	Kansas Power & Light
Boston Edison	Montana Power
Carolina Pr. & Lt.	Niagara Mohawk Power
Central Hudson G. & E.	Pacific Gas & Electric
Central Ill. Pub. Serv.	Pennsylvania Pr. & Lt.
Cincinnati Gas & Electric	Potomac Electric Power
Cleveland Elec. Illum.	Public Service of Colorado
Columbus & So. Ohio	Southern California Edison
Commonwealth Edison	Union Electric
Consolidated Edison	Wisconsin Electric Power
Consumers Power	
Dayton Pr. & Lt.	*Holding Companies*
Detroit Edison	Allegheny Power
Duke Power	American Electric Power
Duquesne Light	Central & South West
Idaho Power	General Public Utilities
Illinois Power	Middle South Utilities
Indianapolis Pr. & Lt.	Southern Company
Kansas City Pr. & Lt.	Texas Utilities

There are several points of comparison you should make before selecting a utility stock. First, compare the price-earnings ratios. All other things being equal, choose the one with the lowest P/E. Next compare the yields. By looking at the Standard & Poor's "yellow cards," available in almost any broker's office or public library, you can determine which utility has recently applied for a rate increase or recently been granted one. Also included in the yellow card will be the annual growth rate in electric power consumption for the area the company serves. You should also check the company's plans for new financing, which will be outlined on the yellow card. In times of high interest rates, preference should be given to companies with less financing immediately ahead.

Nuclear Power Poses Problems

Only a few years ago, most observers thought that by this time all new electric power plants would be fueled by nuclear energy. Eventually, of course, they will have to be, because there simply is not enough fossil fuel left in the earth, nor is there enough clean air for people to breathe, even with precipitators on the utilities' smoke stacks. But the investor should be at least a little wary of any utility with extensive plans for large nuclear fuel plants, because long delays in building—such as those caused by public apprehension over the safety of the plants and those caused by environmental groups—can be very costly to the company.

Of course, there is just as great a problem today in finding locations for conventional power plants. Here too, the objection of environmental groups—just or unjust, as the case may be—has been a delaying factor in the expansion of many utilities. Another problem the utilities must now cope with is the demand, made into law in many states, that only fuel with a low sulfur content be burned. There simply isn't enough low-sulfur fuel available to meet these demands. As a result, sharply higher fuel costs are possible. But, as noted, the demand for electrical power remains so compelling that whatever increases in costs the companies face will probably be offset by fair rates for electricity. Labor costs, it should be emphasized, are not the problem for utilities that they are for most industrials. The ratio of wages to revenues is lower for the electric utilities than it is for any other industry.

Growth Rate vs. P/E

Usually an above-average growth rate is more likely to appeal to investors than is a below-average price-earnings ratio. But in the case of the utilities, investors should not be beguiled by the growth rates of utilities in fast-expanding areas such as Florida, Texas, Arizona, and Southern California, particularly since these fast-growth utilities are usually accorded much higher P/E ratios than other utilities. The slower-growth utilities have the advantages of a lower P/E (which usually also means a higher dividend yield) and the greater likelihood of rate increases. When you add the high yield to the long-term capital gain likely from even the slowest growing utilities, the total return is apt to be greater than what you get by adding the lower yield of the rapid-growth utilities to their likely capital gain (much of which is already discounted in the higher P/E). In fewer words, you may find that better opportunities exist in slower-growth utilities because of their lower price-earnings ratios.

QUESTIONS AND ANSWERS

Q. Why is a reduction in the banks' prime lending rate bullish for utility stocks?

A. There are two reasons why it *might* be, all other things being equal: (1) When interest rates drop, the cost of borrowing money drops. Utilities are huge borrowers of money to finance the expansion of electric power capacity. (2) Most investors think of utilities as high current income stocks. When interest rates drop, bonds and preferred stocks tend to go up. As this happens, they offer less "competition" for utility stocks.

Q. Why would anyone want to buy a utility preferred stock that is not convertible into common stock? Is there any advantage? I can't see any.

A. Neither can I. For individual investors, the simple preferred stock is a cross between a common stock and a bond, with the disadvantages of both and the advantages of neither. Therefore, one should buy a simple preferred stock only when it is an overwhelming bargain—which is unlikely in the case of a utility. For corporations, however, there is a big advantage in buying preferred stocks for income: Corporations must pay a tax on only 15% of dividends received from other U. S. corporations, whereas 100% of any bond interest is taxable at the usual corporate rate.

11

HOW TO MAKE A "DOUBLE PLAY" IN CONVERTIBLE BONDS

If you buy the right ones at the right time, convertible bonds are a way of having your cake and eating it too. More specifically, they offer the investor a way of playing the stock market for capital gains without taking all the risks of owning common stock.

Since they are bonds, they are usually less risky to hold than stocks. But since they are convertible into a specified number of shares of common stock at specified prices, they can go up in price when the common stock goes up. Another attraction is that the coupons on the bond often provide a higher current return on the investment than do the dividends on the stock. Finally, convertible bonds can usually be bought on lower margin (less money down) than the going margin requirement for common stock. By buying convertibles on margin, therefore, you can sometimes get more leverage on your investment than by buying common stock.

In recent years the supply of convertibles has increased, and so has the variety of them you can choose from. They have become a convenient way for corporations to raise money without paying as high an interest rate as they would have to pay on ordinary bonds or bank loans. The conversion feature makes these bonds more attractive, and investors are therefore willing to buy them at yields that are somewhat below the going rates on most comparable non-convertible corporate bonds.

When to Buy Convertibles

The ideal time to buy a convertible bond for possible capital gains is when it is selling at a substantial discount from its face value as a bond, and when there is a good chance that the stock into which it is convertible will rise appreciably over the coming year or two. Not any convertible bond will do, of course. The company has to be financially sound and clearly always able to pay the interest on its outstanding bonds and other debts. Otherwise, the bond would be no less risky than the common stock.

The fact that a $1,000 bond is selling at a discount doesn't necessarily mean there is anything wrong with the bond as a debt security. There have been long periods when you could look down the list of New York Stock Exchange bonds in the financial pages of your newspaper, and find bonds of many of the best-known blue-chip companies selling at less than 100 (100 means $1,000). Especially during periods of very tight money, prices of high-grade bonds may dip down into the 80's or 70's, or even the 60's, depending upon the coupon rate of the bond and the maturity date. The ones with lower coupon rates, such as 4 percent, will naturally dip lower than those with 5 percent or 6 percent rates or higher, and the ones that mature twenty years from now will dip lower than those that mature in only a few years (at which time they are cashed in for $1,000 each).

The *double play* in convertible bonds develops when the price of the bond declines to a discount from par (100). This is usually a period of tight money, when the whole bond market is depressed, and it is also likely to be a period of depressed stock prices. At such times you can buy certain convertibles that have two things going for them at once: They might go up if the bond market goes up, simply because they are bonds, even if the stocks into which they are convertible go down. And if the stocks go up, the bonds might go up with them, even if bonds generally stand still or go down. In effect, then, you are making two guesses at once—that bonds generally will go up, and that the particular stock into which your bond is convertible will go up. If either guess turns out to be right, you have a capital gain. This certainly puts the odds in your favor. Before we illustrate the double play, however, let's look at an example of a straight play in convertible bonds.

A Convertible Success Story

Suppose that you are attracted by the growth potential of a company called International Mind-Expanding Drugs, Inc. (fictional, of course). The stock is selling at 40 on the Big Board and pays a dividend of $1.20. Just about the time when you are about to buy the stock, the company announces that it is planning to issue $20 million worth of convertible debentures, and will use the money to retire its short-term bank loans and to finance more research on mind-expanding drugs. The announcement of the coming financing makes the stock sell off to 38, as often happens. The stock remains in the 37–39 area until the new bonds come onto the market.

The bonds have a 5½ percent coupon rate, at a time when most corporate bonds of this high quality yield 7 percent. The conversion terms are that the bond is convertible at any time between now and twenty years from now, when it matures, into 25 shares of common stock at $40 a share. The bond begins trading at 100, which means $1,000, and is quickly bid up to a slight premium, say 103, while the stock remains at 38.

At this point, the conversion value, or stock value, of the bond is 25 times 38, or $950 (95). However, due to the growth potential of the stock and the fact that the 5½ percent coupon provides a higher current return than does the $1.20 annual dividend on the stock, investors are willing to pay slightly more for the bond than what it is worth on a convertibility basis.

You, too, are willing to pay 103 for the bond, and you call up your broker and tell him, "Buy me five International Mind-Expanding 5½'s of 1992 at market." The order goes through at 103 per bond. Your broker is one of the biggest brokerage houses, and you leave the bonds in your account. In the back of your mind is the general idea that some time within the next two years, when the Food and Drug Administration gives its approval to the company's new line of seven mind expanders, the stock will have a sharp run-up, because this is the kind of news that turns the institutional investors on. As the stock goes up, the bond will go up with it. In fact, since each bond is convertible into 25 shares of stock, the bond will go up 2½ points for every point the stock goes up.

However, as sometimes happens to stocks you think might go up in a couple of years, the stock begins going up the very next day. It goes up to 42 on heavy volume the following day (the institutions have suddenly discovered it) and by the end of the following week it is up to 50. The bond, rising in unison with the stock, is now 126, which is just a one-point premium over its conversion value.

By this time all the chartists in the country have gotten their buy signals, and all the financial publications are full of talk about the long-term profit potentials of mind-expanding drugs. The volume of trading in the stock soars, and the stock makes a number of wild fluctuations. The bond fluctuates with it. At one point, however, the fluctuations stop and the stock goes straight up into orbit, as it were. Within six weeks, the stock is selling at 90 and the bond is 225.

You now have a gain of about 122 percent on your investment, and being a cautious fellow, you decide to nail it down by selling the five bonds at 225. You congratulate yourself on your foresight, and put the money into other convertibles that haven't moved yet.

Postscript: About two months later, the stock hits a high of 150, and the bond reaches 375! But don't fret. You never can guess the exact top or the exact bottom. At least you came out ahead.

A Double Play: Case History

Suppose that the country has been through a period of very tight money, in which the entire bond market has been weak. Many convertible bonds with coupon rates of 6 percent are selling in the 70's and 80's. You are particularly interested in the growth prospects of a company named General Flying Belts, Inc. Although the company's products have never gotten off the ground, you have reason to believe they soon will. Two years ago the company issued some 6 percent convertible debentures, which were convertible into fifty shares of common stock at 20. At that time the stock was selling for 17. Since then, the apparent failure of the company to develop its product line resulted in a considerable reduction in the company's cash position and substantial operating losses. The stock plummeted to 7. The bond, hit by the combination of a generally weak bond market plus the weakening of the company's financial situation (which nevertheless remains strong enough to rule out bankruptcy) fell all the way down to 50, where it yields a whopping 12 percent. But it has a conversion value of only 35, since the stock is only 7.

You study the situation and come to the conclusion that the bond can't go anywhere from here but up. The company is not in serious trouble. The 12 percent yield on the bond looks secure. And you just know that those flying belts will be perfected in another year or two, and that could make the stock go to 100 (in which case the bond would sell at 500). So you take a flyer and buy two of the bonds, for a total cost of $1,000 ($500 each).

The double play, in this situation, is working for you. And this is what happens. About a month after you buy the bonds, the company announces that it is going out of the flying belt business. It simply cannot solve the technological problems involved, and does not want to squander any more of its stockholders' money trying to make flying belts that fly. It will henceforth concentrate its efforts on what for years has been its principle bread-and-butter item: the production and distribution of women's brassieres.

The effect of the announcement is an immediate sell-off in the stock, as disillusioned mutual fund managers dump hundreds of thousands of shares now that the stock is devoid of all glamour. The stock, by the end of the week, is selling at 5½. But the bond—and here is where the double play possibility saves you—moves up sharply on the announcement, and ends the week at 66, where its current yield (now 9.3 percent) is more in line with other bonds. The ending of the financial drain caused by attempting to develop the flying belts made the bond look much better to investors. Furthermore, the whole bond market rallied that week, after months of decline, and the General Flying Belts convertibles went up with the other bonds, simply because they were depressed bonds, as well as because of the halt in the company's staggering R&D expenses. In short, you made 16 points on the bond, or 32 percent.

Convertible Bonds and Leverage

There have been times when it has been possible to buy convertibles and then hock them at the bank. I know of one instance where a group of big traders was able, in effect, to buy a huge stack of the convertible bonds of a major blue-chip company on only 5 percent margin. These traders used the bonds as collateral for a bank loan, and borrowed up to 95 percent of their market value. As it turned out, these traders had advance information on a very favorable corporate development that was pending. When the bullish announcement appeared on the ticker tape, the stock went up about 30 percent, the bonds went up with the stock, and the traders, by having put only 5 percent down, made a profit of 600 percent on their investment instead of just 30 percent.

At present, the Federal Reserve sets margin requirements for both stock purchases and bond purchases. Usually, the margin requirement for convertible bonds is more liberal than for stock. When the difference in margin requirements is big enough, it is sometimes possible to increase the leverage on your investment by buying convertible bonds on margin. But this will work only when the bond is selling at, or very close to, its conversion value. If it sells at a substantial premium over conversion value—which is sometimes the case with bonds selling at discounts from their face value as bonds—the leverage tends to disappear.

Example: ABC convertible bonds are selling at 70. The stock is selling at 25. The bonds are convertible into 20 shares of stock at 50. (These, obviously, are bonds that were issued at a time when the stock was higher than it is now.) You can see at a glance that the conversion value of the bond is 20 times 25, or $500, or 50. If the stock doubled, the conversion value would be 100. At 70, the bond sells at a 40 percent premium over its conversion value, mainly because it is worth about $700 as a straight bond.

In such a situation, if you expected the stock to go up, you would get better leverage just buying the stock. Chances are that as the stock went up the premium on the bond would decrease, thus slowing down the rise in the bond. If the stock doubled and hit 50, the bond might simply go up to 100, the conversion value. At that point, the stock would have doubled while the bond only went up about 43 percent. You would have been much better off buying the stock than the bond.

Convertibles for Hedging

There are a number of ways to hedge your bets on Wall Street, and, in some instances, the effect of the hedging is to limit your possible losses to a very small percentage of the total bet. Traders who operate on a big scale have done this using convertible bonds as a hedge against short sales.

Suppose, for example, that you expect a stock to go down over the coming weeks or months. You are tempted to sell it short, but you realize how risky short-selling is. However, the company has a convertible bond outstanding, which is selling very close to its conversion value, and also very close to its value as a straight bond. This bond gives you an oportunity to sell the stock short and hedge against serious losses by buying the bond. When you have made both these transactions—a short sale on the stock, and a purchase of the convertible bonds—and the number of shares you sold short is about equal to the number of shares the bonds are convertible into, you are well-hedged. The worst that could happen is nothing; that is, the stock and bond stay where they are, and your money has been tied up to no avail. But since speculative stocks seldom stay where they are for very long, even this possibility is remote.

If the stock goes down, the bond probably will not go down with it because it is already selling at about its investment worth as a straight bond. You therefore cover your short sale at a profit, and dispose of the bond at practically no loss. You come out ahead. If your short sale idea turns out to be all wrong and the stock goes up instead of down, the bond goes up with it, so what you lose on the short sale you gain on the bond investment. You guessed wrong, but hardly lost a thing!

It should be stressed, of course, that there are other ways to hedge your bets in the stock market. Call options serve as a hedge against short selling, while put options are a hedge against long positions. In either case, the most you can lose if you have guessed wrong is the cost of the put or call, plus brokerage commissions. And if you are right on your guesses, your profits are almost as much as they would have been on an ordinary stock purchase or short sale.

Hedge funds (which haven't been too successful at hedging so far) try to hedge their bets in another way. They simply have long positions in a group of stocks they think will go up, and short positions in stocks they think will go down. If the market as a whole goes up, the chances are their long positions will show a gain. If the market goes down, chances are they will be ahead on the shorts. And if the market more or less stands still, and their selections have been shrewd enough, they may come out ahead at both ends.

Investors with large portfolios often try to do at least a little hedging. In addition to the techniques mentioned before, they may even try to hedge their long positions by owning a certain amount of gold or silver mining stocks, since these stocks, in the past, have tended to rise in bear markets. But the use of convertible bonds as a hedge against short sales, provided that the bond is close to both its conversion value and its investment worth, is one of the few hedging methods that can almost completely eliminate possible losses.

Stick to the Listed Ones

The market is apt to be somewhat thin in some convertible bonds, and for this reason it is sometimes a bit risky to buy and sell "at the market," without first getting bid and asked quotations from the broker. If the bid and asked prices are only one or two points apart, there is no problem. You can buy at the market if you are in a hurry. But in some instances, especially in the case of unlisted convertibles, there is likely to be a much larger spread. During periods when the bond market is suffering from tight money, the spread may be as much as ten points. If you have to sell in a hurry for some reason, you may get much less for the bond than you thought.

One way to reduce the risk of a thin market and a wide spread is to stick to those convertibles that are listed on the New York Stock Exchange's bond trading list. These bonds are usually more marketable, and they are also likely to be of better quality. And you can follow the price trends every day in the newspaper.

Some Respectable Convertible Bonds

The following list of selected convertible bonds of well-known and firmly-entrenched companies will give you some ideas, if you are interested in this type of investment. Watch them, and whenever they are selling *well below* par (100), they should be good long-term investments:

Alcoa 5¼%, 1991
American Broadcasting 5%, 1993
Crane Co. 5%, 1993
General Telephone 5%, 1992
W. R. Grace 4¼%, 1990
Macy 4¼%, 1990
Miles Labs 5¼%, 1994
North American Philips 4%, 1992
RCA 4½%, 1992
Union Pacific 4¾%, 1999
Xerox 6%, 1995

QUESTIONS AND ANSWERS

Q. I recently purchased five convertible bonds of a large real estate investment trust (REIT). They were priced to yield 6½% and at that price were only slightly above their conversion value. They seemed a good buy, especially in view of the growth prospects of the common stock into which they are convertible. Yet the bonds are already down 10% in price, just three weeks after I bought them. Is there anything wrong with them?

A. What you are really asking is, why did the bonds go down after you bought them? I suspect the main reason is that even though they were yielding 6½% at your purchase price, they were yielding less than the company's common stock was. Don't forget that REITs pay out all their earnings as dividends. Therefore, these stocks have high yields—in this case around 9% for the current year. With the common stock yielding that much more than the convertible bond, it isn't too surprising that the bond went down. In a sense, the two securities are in competition with each other.

Q. What do you think of mutual funds that specialize in convertible bonds and convertible preferred stocks?

A. Generally speaking, such funds are good bets and should be able to offer both high current yield and capital appreciation. They can be bought over a period of time, via dollar averaging, and should be safer than most common stock funds— if they are run intelligently.

12

HOW TO WIN IN OTHER "GAMES" —OPTIONS, WARRANTS, AND COMMODITIES

The stock and bond markets are not the only games in town. Temperamentally, some professional people are more suited to the horse races or a weekend in Las Vegas than to what, for them, is the plodding pace of Wall Street. And why not? If you're a young doctor or dentist with the expectation of many years of lucrative practice before you, minimal responsibilities and a few thousand you don't really need, what's to stop you from gambling with it if you like? Certainly, anyone who takes pen in hand to write a book about the stock market has no business adopting a moral stand on gambling. It's all a gamble, when you come down to it. All we're trying to do is show you how to play with the odds somewhat in your favor. That can also be done in markets where the action is a lot steamier than the New York Stock Exchange. If you play them, though, do so with your eyes wide open. There are no sure-thing bets; if the reward potential looks great, you can be sure that the risk will be equally great.

You Can Opt for Options

We have already touched on the option market as a means of hedging in the stock market, but it also has other uses—mainly sheer speculation.

The rules are very simple. When you buy an option, what you are doing is purchasing the right to buy or sell a stock at today's price at some time in the future. There are three kinds of options: calls, puts and straddles. A call gives you the right to buy the stock at any time before the term of the option—normally 30 days, 60 days or 195 days. The longer the term, the higher the price of the option; note that a 195-day term gives you leeway to take a long-term capital gain. A put gives you the right to sell, and with a straddle you win if the stock moves either way. Of course, it has to move far enough to cover the cost of the option, which in the case of a straddle usually will be about twice as high as a put or a call.

For a look at the profit potential of options, let's take an actual case. Five months before this was written, Control Data common was selling at 44½, but an option dealer in New York offered a six month call on the stock at 41½ for $787.50. More recently, Control Data has been selling at 58½. Suppose, with the benefit of hindsight, we had known that it was going to go up that much. At the time the margin requirement was 75 percent, so we could have bought 100 shares for $3,342. By now we would have a paper profit of $1,400, or not quite 42 percent. Not bad.

But suppose, instead, we had bought four calls on Control Data—for a little less money than we had to put up to buy the stock on margin. They would have cost $3,152, but we could have made 17 points on each, or $6,800. Subtracting their cost, we would have come out with a clear profit—disregarding commissions—of $3,648, a gain of 115 percent.

All very well, but let's assume that, instead of going up, Control Data had gone down 14 points. By buying the stock, we'd have lost $1,400, or 42 percent of our investment. But, by buying the call instead, we'd have lost the entire $3,152, or 100 percent of our investment.

In sum, buying options is a method of achieving maximum leverage at a time when margin requirements are high. As in any leverage situation, the risks are proportionate to the potential gain. Because stock prices go down much faster than they go up, puts usually beat calls as a speculation medium. It's all a question of timing. If you're convinced that the top of a bull market has been reached and the inevitable plunge is at hand, buy some puts on very high-multiple stocks, the speculative favorites of the moment. If you're right about sighting the bear, the payoff will be spectacular.

As for straddles, don't bother with them. If you don't have good reason to believe that a stock is going to move up or down, and a firm conviction about which way, there's no sense buying an option on it in the first place. On the other hand, it sometimes makes sense to sell them.

And that brings us to the third way to use options. (No. 1 was as a means of hedging, remember? And No. 2 was to satisfy your gambling lust with a fixed input of money, so that if you lose the loss will be no more than you decided in advance you could afford.) The third alternative, "writing" options yourself, makes the most sense. It's a practical way to make money in the stock market, a bit like being on the side of the house in a gambling casino. When you buy an option from an option broker, remember that he is just that, a broker. Someone else is selling because he expects to make a profit on it, and the chances are that he will come out very well indeed.

Harold Starr, of the San Francisco firm of Starr & Kuehl, who is one of the pioneers of the option business in this country, says that anyone with a feel for the stock market who learns the techniques of writing options should be able to realize 30 percent on invested capital annually, with a minimum of risk. "What you should do," he says, "is set your sights on 30 percent, but don't be disappointed if you make 20 percent." That, he emphasizes, is after taxes.

The first step is to open an account with an option broker who specializes in that field, or the option department of a brokerage house that does. In the latter case, it should be a firm that has a liberal policy on options—in contrast with one major firm which requires a $500,000 deposit when opening an option account. A liberal firm requires only $2,000 and permits the writing of "naked" options—meaning that you don't necessarily have to own the stock in order to write a call on it, or have a short position in it for a put. Among the liberal firms on Wall Street in this respect are Merrill Lynch, Reynolds & Co. and Burr Wilson. The latter is a relatively small firm which, nevertheless, has a large option business.

In opening such an account, in effect you hang out your shingle as an option writer. No further publicity is necessary. Within a short time the broker will be calling you: "Do you want to write a call on PDQ Corp. for ninety days for $200 at 30?" You look up the stock. It's selling at 28 and there seems no good reason for the price to rise, but it's a volatile stock and might jump in any direction. You say yes, you'll do it.

Now, one of three things can happen. Either the stock goes up, or it goes down, or it just sits there doing nothing. In the first case, you worry. You've got a margin of four points before you're hurt—the two between 28, where it stands now, and the 30 "strike" quotation, the price at which you've agreed to sell the stock three months hence, plus the two points leeway you have on your $200. Anywhere above 32 you're losing money. So, if it reaches 32 and there seems good reason for it to go higher, you go into the open market and buy 100 shares, hold it until the buyer exercises his option, and sell him the stock at 32. You will have lost some commission money and the interest you would have made by keeping your money in the bank for ninety days, but you're not really bleeding. Where you can get hurt is if, after you buy in, the stock goes down again to, say, 28 before the ninety days is out. Then, you will have lost $400, minus the $200 you received for the option, or $200 plus commissions.

But let's look on the bright side. If PDQ Corp. just sits at 28 or goes down, you've made $200 on no investment in ninety days. Well, if you figure your $2,000 deposit in the option account as an investment, that's an annual rate of return of 40 percent.

What are the odds? In 1960, the Securities and Exchange Commission made a study of the option market and found that only 54 percent of the puts and calls that are bought are ever exercised. And only 12 percent to 15 percent of those are exercised at a profit. Thus, it's almost a 10-to-1 shot that you'll make money by writing an option. How much you make, of course, depends on how cagey you are in picking the ones you write. Harry Starr says, "There's an old saying in this business that the option buyer is always right. What he thinks is going to happen usually will happen—but not when he thinks it will happen. His timing is almost always wrong."

The tax aspects of option writing are important if you're in a high income bracket. Any profit you make on an option of less than six months duration, of course, is a short-term capital gain. Also, if you write an option for, say, six months and ten days, and the buyer decides to exercise it before the end of that time, but still at a price that will leave you a profit, such a profit is a short-term. On the other hand, proving a long-term capital gain is not simply a matter of writing an option of more than six months duration. The IRS has held that it is long-term if the stock itself has been held for six months; in that case the amount of the premium you receive for the option can be counted as reducing the price at which you bought the stock.

The way to work it, according to Harry Starr, is to dollar average, concentrating on about ten stocks that are "optionable"—in demand from option buyers. You buy, say, $1,000 worth of those 10 stocks every month for a period of time, during which they go up from an average $30 per share to $50. Your average is now $40, so you write calls on them for six months and ten days at $40. The premiums you get for the options, normally amounting to $400 on each 100 shares, will be counted for tax purposes as reducing your average cost to $36. Therefore, each such $400 is a long-term capital gain.

Where option writing becomes a matter of real skill, Harry points out, is in knowing when to buy. Remember that, normally, the buyer of the option had a reason for his action—grounds for thinking, if he bought a call, that the stock would go up. But, just as normally, his timing will be faulty. Thus, according to Harry Starr's observations, what usually happens is that, in the few days or weeks after the option is written, the stock will rise. Then, a reaction will set in and it will drop a point or two below the level at which it was written, then rise again. Says Harry: "A real pro in this business never buys a stock when he writes an option. He waits and watches. Sometime before the option reaches term, the stock will fall back. That's when he buys."

Another thing to remember is that there's a lot of "in-house" trading in options by brokers, usually not to the advantage of their customers. In other words, your broker will get a call from a client who wants an option on XYZ at 30 for $300. Rather than going through an option broker to fill the order, the broker will call you and say, "I've got a buyer for XYZ at 30 for $200. Want it?" The odd $100, of course, adds greatly to the broker's commission on the deal. The only way to protect yourself from such greedy little men is to become thoroughly familiar with the market, so you know what the price should be.

Take a Look at Warrants

Another interesting game is investing in warrants, which can be a good deal more lively than stocks. Run your finger down the list of Big Board stocks in your evening newspaper. Occasionally a stock is listed twice, the second time at a much lower price, and on the second listing the symbol "wt" follows the name of the company. That is the quotation for the warrant, not the stock itself.

Frequently, when a company is raising money via a public stock offering, it will sell not just common shares, but common shares with warrants attached. They are like options, giving the holder the right to buy shares at some future time at today's price. The term, however, is usually for a number of years and the price substantially higher than today's. National Taxidermy, for example, might float an issue of common at 45, although the stock heretofore hasn't been selling that high; to make it more attractive to investors, it will carry a detachable warrant giving the holder the right to buy an additional share at 50 any time in the next five years. After the issue comes out, stock and warrants will trade separately—the stock at 42, say, and the warrants at 3.

If and when the stock moves up in price, the warrant will move faster, percentage-wise. Thus, if National Taxidermy reaches 50, for a gain of 19 percent, it's likely that the warrant will go to 5—for a 66 percent jump. If the stock continues to go up and reaches 60, the warrant probably would move at least to 12. At that point, the investor who bought the warrant when it was first issued has a 300 percent gain, whereas the man who bought the stock has realized a profit of only 42 percent.

When speculating in warrants, bear in mind that there isn't any percentage in buying them when the stock is selling much above the price at which the warrants can be exercised. At that point, they usually move in close relationship to the price of the stock. It's only when the element of risk is great that the return is great. Of course, on the way down warrants also move faster than the stock, as a rule.

One final warning: watch the expiration date. If, say, six months before the last day on which the warrant can be converted into stock, National Taxidermy is back down to 42, the chances are that the warrant will be selling for 50 cents.

The Wide, Wide World of Commodities

Probably the most popular vehicle for speculation, other than the stock market itself, is the commodities market. Over the past ten years, the number of commodity futures contracts written annually has increased from eight million to 29 million. Everybody's doing it, chiefly because of the appeal of the leverage factor. Ordinarily, when you buy a future on a commodity, you're required to put up only about 10 percent of its market value, as compared with 50 percent to 70 percent for stocks, depending on the whim of the Federal Reserve. Moreover, you don't pay interest on the balance, since a future contract is not really an equity; it's more like an option. Suppose, for example, you decide to take a flyer in the wheat market. You buy a contract for 5,000 bushels of wheat, to be delivered to you July 1, at $1.45 per bushel. If it were actually delivered it would cost you $7,250, but for the contract you put up only $725. If, between now and July 1, wheat goes to $1.50 per bushel, which can happen in one day of hard trading on the Chicago Board of Trade, you've made $250 on your $725 investment— a 34 percent gain.

Of course, if wheat goes down, say, 10 cents a bushel, you'll surely get a notice from your broker asking for additional margin. If you don't get it up quickly, they sell your contract for what it will bring.

You can buy or sell futures contracts on a wide variety of commodities—wheat, corn, oats, soybeans, broilers, plywood, silver, cattle, fresh eggs, potatoes, pork bellies (slabs of bacon), hogs, lumber, copper, sugar, wool, orange juice, platinum, and cotton. And that's only a partial list. New markets in commodities are being created all the time. Recently, for example, the Los Angeles Commodities Exchange started trading in bags of silver coins.

An important drawback to commodities trading is that any capital gains you make are likely to be short-term and therefore taxable at the short-term rate. That is because trends in commodity prices usually are short-term. If a stock is fundamentally sound and there's a demand for it, the chances are it will move steadily upward, despite fluctuations caused by profit-taking or general market conditions, over a period of at least six months. But not so with commodities. A trend in wheat, corn or copper may last only a few days or weeks. People who make money in commodities do so on a day-to-day basis. They go long in the morning and, if there's an upward movement of a few points, they may sell out and go short in the afternoon.

It's quite possible to make a lot of money fast in the commodities markets, but you have to know what you're doing. Don't dabble. Particularly disastrous, as a rule, is jumping into a commodity investment on a rumor or crop report of some kind, without investigating to find out whether: (1) the report is true, and (2) whether, if it is true, it will have the anticipated effect. You hear a report on the eleven o'clock news, for example, that there's a heavy frost in Florida, so bright and early the next morning you put in an order for some frozen orange juice futures; the frost, you reason, will cause a shortage and the price will go up. The trouble is that all over the country would-be tycoons like yourself have heard the same report and had the same idea. By the time your order is executed, the market already has gone up the limit of $5. Sometime during the afternoon, word reaches the trading floor that growers got their smudge pots out in time and damage to the Florida orange crop was minimal. The $5 rise in the market will be cancelled out in a matter of minutes—and you're left holding the orange squeezer.

A hundred things can affect the price of a commodity—changes in the supply, changes in demand, government programs to support the price—or, on occasion, dampen it. A leftist takes over the government of Chile and the price of copper shoots sky-high; speculators figure—correctly, as it turns out—that he will nationalize the mines there and that production will then decline. There's an international monetary crisis, gold is shooting up in London, Paris and Zurich, and you, smarty that you are, load up on silver futures. Your reasoning is that whenever the value of the money is called into question, precious metals, including silver, provide a means of protection. People will be buying silver, and the price will go up. The trouble is that the government picks that particular moment to release a large quantity of the metal from its stockpile. Or worse, large silver users, fearing a runaway market, gang up on the market with heavy short selling. It is well to remember, in commodities trading, that the markets are not as well policed as Wall Street; rigging a commodity market is a fairly common occurrence.

Here are some tips from an experienced commodity trader:

—Watch your expiration dates. Unless you have a very large waiting room, it may get a little crowded when a truck drives up and delivers the 5,000 bushels of soybeans you ordered last April.

—Trade in commodities only with genuine risk capital. You can't play this market with scared money, only sums that you can afford to lose.

—Forget any hangups you may have about selling short. Anyone who makes money in commodity markets is short at least as often as he is long.

—Concentrate on a few commodities and learn all about them. It's a mistake to spread yourself too thin from a standpoint of research.

—Don't hand your money over to any self-styled expert in commodities to invest for you on a discretionary basis. If he really were an expert, he wouldn't need your capital; he could make plenty by trading for his own account.

—Look at all the factors. Our expert says: "I'm about 70 percent fundamentalist and about 30 percent technician. Take soybeans, for example. I look at the basic supply-demand figures; the export picture; the probable harvest; the inventory situation; what domestic usage is going to be; markets for other grains, such as sorghums, wheat and corn, which vie with soybeans for animal feed. I also consider government price support levels. All this adds up to the fundamental aspects of the market. Now I look at the technical aspects, the open interest, the volume and the chart patterns. Only after taking all these factors into consideration do I decide to buy, sell or sit tight. Mostly, unless I find real reasons for doing otherwise, I sit tight."

—Remember that, according to government surveys, 75 percent of the people who trade in commodities lose money.

One With the Profits Built-In

One other off-beat investment medium deserves mention—a sort of commodity.

Can you think of anything you can buy that automatically increases in value with age? Antiques, maybe. But investing in them requires an expertise beyond the ken of most of us. No, this is a common commodity, as familiar as soybeans or orange juice concentrate.

Scotch whisky.

It just lies there in the barrels, safe and sound in a bonded warehouse. And by the simple process of aging it increases in value—ordinarily about 25 percent per year.

And it's as simple as investing in any other commodity, except that you don't get the leverage. No margin accounts. If you buy 1,000 gallons of whisky, you put up the full price. But otherwise, it's strictly a paper transaction. You buy the warehouse receipts through a dealer in this country, and when you decide it's time to sell, he sells them for you at the market in Glasgow.

There are just two factors that make it less than foolproof. One is that the scotch market is like any other—it fluctuates according to the whims of supply and demand. While it is quite true that the intrinsic value of the whisky increases with age, the market value doesn't necessarily do so. To start with, the price you pay for the new booze when it's laid down in the barrels depends on how many other people are bidding for it, and how high they're willing to go. Then, when you want to sell, buyer demand depends on the amounts available to the blenders and how well Scotch is selling around the world at that particular moment and also on the market for competing liquors. Right now, Scotch exporters are warily eying the new American light whiskies—will they cut into the demand for Scotch? As a consequence, four-year-old grains in Scotland are selling not much above the price of newly distilled spirits.

The other difficulty is that of tracking your investment. You can't pick up the *Wall Street Journal* and find today's quote for 18-month-old neutral grain spirits in Glasgow. (Unless you're a real expert, you buy neutral grain rather than blending whiskies; the aging factor is just as important, and you don't have to keep up with blending-room idiosyncracies.) Even in Scotland, only a couple of trade papers keep abreast of the market. Therefore, you're dependent on your broker for quotations, and some of the people making a market in Scotch warehouse receipts in this country are not above falsifying the quotations. Nor can you buy through your regular stockbroker. He probably knows less than you do about this market.

As of this writing, the only dealer in Scotch warehouse receipts in this country who is registered with the SEC is Accrued Equities, 122 East 42nd St., New York, N.Y 10017, which is run by Maurice Schoenwald.

We've raced sailboats with him on Long Island Sound and know him as a man who goes all the way around the buoy, even if no one is looking.

QUESTIONS AND ANSWERS

Q. I am interested in the speculative potential of low-price warrants. For instance, the Atlas Corp. warrants are selling for 1⅜. What are the probabilities?

A. The common stock is only 2⅝, so why buy the warrants, which merely give you the privilege of buying the common for 6¼? The common would have to rise 191% in order to justify the current price of the warrant. You had better forget all about warrants anyhow.

Q. Under what circumstances are warrants good investments?

A. Most warrants are overpriced most of the time. But if you can spot the precise bottom of a long bear market, that is when you can sometimes pick up warrants at a price that will give you a spectacular capital gain. The most famous example, at the bottom of the 1929–1932 bear market, was the Tri-Continental warrants, which, I am told, were selling for 25¢ (they are now around 72).

A study by *Finance* magazine of the relative price action of warrants and their related common stocks during a recent six-month period revealed that some warrants did considerably better than the common stock. For instance, the AT&T common rose 20% during this period, while the warrant rose 51%. Similarly, the Fiberboard common rose 49% but the warrant rose 91%. However, the study also picked up examples of the common stock doing better than the warrant. The Tenneco common rose 33%, while the warrant rose only 6%. The Atlantic Richfield common rose 17%, while the warrant declined 11%.

13

TAX-SHELTERED INVESTMENTS FOR THE PROFESSIONAL MAN*

Most professional men are aware, at least vaguely, that there are such things as tax-sheltered investments other than state and municipal bonds, but there is a general impression that they were no longer attractive after passage of the Tax Reform Act of 1969. The year after it passed, a New York City area physician who for five years previously had been making sizable profits in oil drilling funds, wrote to us that he had decided against going into any more such ventures.

"I was in on a project that couldn't have been better," he wrote wistfully. "It made several quick strikes and started producing profits the first year. In four years I had my original investment back, at least on paper. Then it went public, and in six years the stock went from $9 to a high of $54, and I sold at the peak.

But now I can't see oil drilling funds. First, the funds going public now aren't making the grade. The price-earnings ratio is off for the whole industry. And if you convert to cash, the cash surrender value will be much less than the value according to the oil reserves, because of the complicated formula they use to appraise the reserves.

If I were to put $10,000 in a drilling fund now, it would really amount to a $5,000 investment because I'm in the 50 percent bracket. Uncle Sam pays the rest. But there is no liquidity. I have no assurance that they will strike oil, no assurance they will convert my investment to common stock, and no assurance the stock will rise.

Now, if I put $5,000 into high-grade corporate bonds at 9 percent, I know that at the end of the year I'll have $5,450, and what's more important, I can take that money out any time I want to. Of course, a lot of physicians will see half their income going to the government and want that tax shelter. But I personally feel that the days of the really big profits from oil drilling funds are over."

That was in August, 1970. With the benefit of hindsight, let's see if the author of the letter was right. In fact, he didn't do badly; in the following year the price of his bonds went up, so that his effective yield on them was more like 15 percent than 9

* By Robert Johnson

percent. On the other hand, many of the drilling funds turned in particularly good results that year. Serio Exploration Co., for example, reported that participants in its 1970 A-1 program benefited from a major discovery, the Stamps Field in Wilkinson County, Mo., and by the following year they were reaping an annual 18 percent return. Adobe Corp.'s 1970 program was yielding a sensational 23 percent. Since the income from such investments is subject to the 22 percent depletion allowance, and virtually all drilling costs must be recovered before any tax liability is incurred, participants obviously were making much more money on their investments than the man who put his savings into corporate bonds. Of course, the latter had the advantages of almost negligible risk and greater liquidity.

Opportunities Still Abound

The fact is that, although the 1969 Tax Reform dimmed, to a small extent, the glamour of tax-sheltered investments, they remain exceedingly attractive for professional men who are in a 50 percent tax bracket or higher. Indeed, some important new opportunities have been opened up, particularly in the home construction field. The Federal Housing Administration's 236 program, designed to foster the construction of large numbers of homes for low-income groups, offers extraordinary incentive to investors.

Shortly before we went to press, there was a freeze on the funding of the 236 program, and the future of it was not clear. But the 236 program (Section 236 of the National Housing Act of 1968) provides for federal rent subsidies to low-income tenants, so that in effect their rent is 30 percent to 35 percent lower than the going rate in the areas selected for such developments. This results in almost 100 percent occupancy of the homes or apartment houses, and since the mortgages are FHA-insured the risk to investors is almost nil. Moreover, while the 1969 Tax Reform Act barred the use of the double-declining balance method of depreciation for most real estate, it specifically exempted residential rental property. Also, if the property is sold to the tenants under some kind of cooperative arrangement after a few years, payment of income tax on any capital gain accruing to the investor can be delayed for one year, or indefinitely if it is reinvested in another low-income housing project.

The way 236 projects usually work is that ten limited partners put up $50,000 each, payable in installments over a period of a year to eighteen months. Their $500,000 supports mortgage financing of $3.3 million. Large tax losses are incurred during the initial construction phase, since there is no rental income and the entire burden of interest on the construction loan, real estate taxes, and other deductible items falls upon the limited partners. Also, in the first few years of operation, accelerated depreciation and high interest costs mean heavy write-offs. Normally, an investor in the 50 percent tax bracket can expect to recoup all of his investment via tax losses by the third or fourth year. Lesser tax losses will continue to accrue for the first twenty years, assuming a forty-year mortgage. Distributions of income from the project are tax-free, since they constitute a return of capital. Over a period of eleven years, the investor who put up $50,000 should realize a yield of $64,600 beyond the return of his initial input.

Finding the "Loopholes"

Tax-sheltered investments often are called "loopholes," implying that the wealthy use them to escape payment of taxes. But the fact is that they exist because Congress wrote them into the law in order to encourage certain types of investments; they weren't created by Congressional oversight. For example, the investment tax credit, which allows businessmen to deduct from their taxes 7 percent of the cost of new machines and other production equipment, was re-instituted at the start of 1972 as a spur to the U.S. economy. It was supposed to boost employment and, at the same time, encourage industry to modernize so that the U.S. could compete more effectively in world markets. Similarly, the depletion allowance which allows oil companies to avoid tax payments on 22 percent of the revenue from producing wells is designed to encourage domestic exploration at a time when an "energy crisis" impends because of a shortage of low-cost fuel. The housing boom which was instrumental in pulling the nation out of the 1970–71 recession was stimulated, to a large extent, by such programs as 236.

Investing money in such a way as to take advantage of these so-called loopholes, therefore, is perfectly legitimate, but it must be done in approved fashion. Some years ago, an officer of a midwestern corporation decided, a bit arbitrarily, to reduce his tax bill. In filling out his tax return, he entered a loss equal to his annual salary which, he said, had been caused by a fire that destroyed his entire stable of polo ponies. In due course, he received a whopping tax refund, but two weeks after it arrived the IRS called him in for an audit. Forced to admit that he had never owned a polo pony, he succeeded in staying out of jail, but he had to pay a huge penalty along with fees for extensive legal services. A casualty loss from a fire that destroys polo ponies you don't own definitely does not qualify as a tax-sheltered investment!

The most important characteristic of such investments is that some portion of the initial outlay may be deducted from ordinary income in the first year. Another is that some part of the future income should be tax-free. A third desirable characteristic is that they should enable the payment of taxes to be deferred from the current year to some time in the future. Finally, a tax-sheltered investment should be ultimately salable at a profit, with the profit to be taxed as a long-term capital gain.

Cattle Breeding: A Bullish View

Let's look at some kinds of tax shelters, leaving until later the technical aspects of tax deductibility and management contracts. One of the most common tax-sheltered investments is cattle breeding, a business into which the government has sought to encourage the flow of risk capital as a means of improving herds. Although the purchase price of a herd of breeding cattle is not tax-deductible, other angles make it possible for an investor in a 50 percent tax bracket to realize a first year deduction about equal to his initial outlay. For openers, about 75 percent of the herd's cost will be borrowed at from ½ percent to 1½ percent above the prime rate, and the interest, of course, is tax-free. Second, the double-declining balance method of depreciation can be used, except in cases where an animal has previously been used for breeding, in which case depreciation is limited to 150 percent of straight-line. Usually, though, this means that 20 percent of the herd's cost can be deducted in the first year. Finally, all expenditures for feed, pasturage, labor, management fees and other costs incidental to raising the animals are deductible as business expense.

Every year, a calf crop equal to about three-quarters of the size of the herd can be expected. The young steers are sold off, while the heifers are retained to build up the herd. Revenue from the steers is taxed as ordinary income; however, each year the herd is culled and the less desirable animals sold; providing they have been held for two years or more, that income is taxed at the capital gains rate. By means of modern genetic techniques, the quality of the herd is built up to increase its value. Within three generations, such methods can add about $75 to the value of the average steer.

Cattle breeding investments work on a five-to-seven year cycle, at the end of which the herd is sold. Profits are taxed at the capital gains rate, except that under the 1969 reform act depreciation deductions must be recaptured by the tax collector; hence, a portion of the gains will be taxed at the ordinary rate. Also, the 1969 act introduced the concept of the Excess Deduction Account (EDA), which affects taxpayers who have non-farm adjusted gross income of $50,000 per year or more; all farm losses of more than $25,000 in any one year must be entered into the EDA, and when the assets are ultimately sold any gain up to the EDA total must be listed as ordinary income. Few cattle breeding enterprises, however, are so large that EDA presents a serious problem for investors.

Cattle feeding operations provide another method of sheltering investments for high-income taxpayers, although no depreciation is allowed, and any profit must be treated as ordinary income. The tax shelter comes about primarily through leverage—about 75 percent of the cost of the young steers is borrowed, and the interest is tax deductible, as is the cost of feed, rental of the feeding lot, etc. Profits result from the weight gained by the young animals because of intensive feeding in the five or six months prior to slaughter.

In a typical program, 100 young steers weighing an average 600 pounds are purchased in July for 33⅓ cents per pound—total $20,000. Of that sum, the investor puts up $5,000 and the bank $15,000. Grain is purchased for a total of $10,000, again financed in the proportion $7,500 by the bank, $2,500 by the investor. Other expenses, including interest, amount to $2,000—divided $1,500 and $500. As of now, the investor has put up $8,000 and has tax-deductible costs of $12,000; if he is in the 50 percent tax bracket, his tax bill for that year will be reduced by $6,000. In January, the steers each weigh 1,000 pounds. Assuming that the price of beef hasn't changed, they are sold for $33,333. After paying off the bank loan of $24,000, the investor recoups his $8,000 investment plus a profit of $1,333, or 16⅔ percent for six months.

Naturally, profits in cattle feeding can be radically affected by the efficiency of the operator and by fluctuations in the price of beef. It is possible to hedge against the latter effectively by simply selling cattle futures short at the time the steers are purchased; then, if the price goes down, the loss will be offset by a profit on the future contract.

Also, it is possible to negotiate a deal with the feed lot operator under which the animals are brought up to a specified weight at a guaranteed cost per pound. Eliminating risks by such means, of course, will reduce the profit potential. Many cattle feeding programs are conducted over five or six year periods; like dollar-averaging in stocks, this tends to level out the swings in cattle prices.

Equipment Leasing as a Shelter

Most other farm shelters, such as citrus groves and vineyards, lost most of their allure in the 1969 tax reform. Costs of planting and cultivating the trees or vines until they reach maturity now must be capitalized, rather than written off as a business expense. In similar fashion, Congress took a lot of the glamour out of equipment leasing in 1971, when it revised the rules applicable to the investment tax credit. Nevertheless, some aspects of equipment leasing are interesting.

Businessmen frequently prefer to lease such items of equipment as airplanes, railroad freight cars and computers rather than buying them, in order to conserve working capital. High-income investors find it advantageous to finance such leases, normally borrowing 80 percent of the cost of the equipment on a non-recourse basis; that is, the credit of the user secures the loan, and if he fails to pay the investor cannot be held accountable. One private investor group on the East Coast forgot this provision and ended up with fifteen large trucks less than a year after they formed the partnership. They were able to re-lease the trucks, but took a sizable loss. Insurance and maintenance also is the responsibility of the user. Interest on the loan, of course, is a tax-deductible expense for the investor, as is depreciation on the equipment, which may be taken on an accelerated basis so as to increase the write-offs in the early years of the lease. Indeed, the 1969 tax reform act made it possible for some equipment—notably railroad rolling stock, some pollution control devices and coal mine safety equipment—to be depreciated over a five-year period. Congress wanted to channel investment funds into those areas.

However, in 1971 Congress changed the rules concerning application of the investment tax credit to equipment leasing. As of this writing, an individual or partnership engaged in leasing may receive the credit only if the term of the lease is less than half the useful life of the asset and first year expenses are more than 15 percent of first year rental income. In effect, this eliminates availability of the investment tax credit for most persons in the equipment leasing business. Moreover, accelerated depreciation in excess of straight line depreciation is an item of tax preference subject to the 10 percent minimum tax. At the expiration of the lease, any profit realized through sale of the asset must be treated as ordinary income for tax purposes. Interest cost now is deductible only up to a ceiling of $25,000. Nevertheless, individuals in high income brackets who are close to retirement age will find equipment leasing an attractive tax shelter which is virtually without risk.

Most of the questions related to tax shelters that professional men have asked us are questions about tax exempt bonds or about tax losses. Here, and at the end of the next chapter, are some samples.

QUESTIONS AND ANSWERS

Q. Would you list the tax advantages of setting up a custodial account for children?

A. There are a number of tax advantages, and you should consult your lawyer for details. Generally speaking, however, when the stocks or other securities are put in a custodial account, they become the child's property. The income tax, if any, is figured at the child's lower rate rather than at your rate. There is also another dividend exclusion permitted. With the increase in personal exemptions under the 1969 tax reform law, as well as additional deductions for low income, this whole procedure is attracting more interest now.

Q. I would appreciate it if you could clarify a problem on which I have been given conflicting advice from several different brokers. One broker tells me that the interest on tax-exempt municipal bonds is always tax-exempt as far as federal taxes are concerned. Another tells me that it is only tax-exempt if you are not claiming any interest you might have paid on any loan or deduction.

I am sure many other physicians would also appreciate your opinion on this. Personally, I feel that there must be very few people indeed who have no loans of any sort. Most have mortgages or auto loans or something of that kind. Can't these people benefit from the tax-exempt income of the bonds?

A. The interest income from tax-exempt municipal bonds is exempt from federal income taxes. It makes no difference how much money you owe the bank on your house, your car, or anything else. However, you cannot borrow money specifically to buy municipal bonds and then deduct both the interest payments on the loan and the interest income from the bonds. But you can still deduct other interest payments, even while you collect your tax-exempt interest income.

Q. I live in Florida and am interested in buying some tax-exempt bonds. Should I stick to Florida bonds rather than those from other states? Would I save on the state income tax that way?

A. If you buy bonds of the State of Florida or of some municipality in Florida, the interest income is exempt from both federal and state taxes. If you buy a bond from another state, the interest would still be exempt from federal taxes, but you would have to pay a state income tax on it (which in turn would be a deduction from your federal tax).

Q. About nine years ago, when First Lincoln Financial Corp. went public (at $21 a share), I bought 180 shares. Dividends have been paid in additional shares, at about 5%, over the years until two years ago. I have sold 100 shares to establish a tax loss and now have 128 shares left. The current bid price, over the counter, is 4¾. The company is offering subscription rights to additional shares at $4 each. A shareholder may also oversubscribe. Should I subscribe to more of these shares?

A. You might consider this scheme: Subscribe to as many additional shares as you can get. Wait 31 days and then sell an equal number of shares from your original batch. That way you get a tax loss on the sale but maintain your equity in the company.

14

TURNING YOUR TAX BILL
INTO AN ASSET*

The most attractive feature of tax-sheltered investments is that a large part of the outlay can be deducted from income, when it comes to totaling up your tax bill in the first year. Normally the deduction will amount to at least 60 percent of the investment, and it may go as high as 100 percent or even 200 percent. This brings the out-of-pocket cost of the investment down appreciably. The following table shows the after-tax cost of a $10,000 investment for an individual in the 60 percent tax bracket for various degrees of first-year deductibility.

	Initial Investment Deductibility		
	60%	100%	200%
Investment	$10,000	$10,000	$10,000
Reduction in taxable income	6,000	10,000	20,000
Tax saving	3,600	6,000	12,000
After-tax cost	6,400	4,000	(2,000)

Note that with 200 percent deductibility, the investor realized an initial tax saving $2,000 greater than his investment. After making the investment, he retained $2,000 more than if he had not gone into the deal at all; in other words, he made money by spending it.

The Use of Leverage

Deductibility in excess of initial investment can be achieved only through leverage—using borrowed money. Oil and gas drilling programs provide the best means of leveraging tax-sheltered investments. To start with, all costs of drilling a well, amounting to 70 percent to 80 percent of the total cost, are immediately deductible in the year that it is drilled, and the cost of any dusters (dry holes) also goes to reduce the investor's tax liability. Moreover, drilling programs frequently are structured in such a way that the sponsor's funds are used for pipe, pumps and other non-deductible equipment,

* By Robert Johnson

119

while the investors pay actual drilling costs. Hence, 100 percent of their input is deductible. Finally, most oil and gas exploration funds are set up not to drill a single well, but to carry out a broad-scale drilling program, frequently in a number of different fields. As soon as some successful wells have been completed, the partnership can use them as collateral for a loan to drill more. In this way, tax deductions greater than the original investments of the participating partners can be obtained. Loans, however, must be on a non-recourse basis, involving no liability to the limited partners, and a partner cannot claim deductions exceeding his contribution plus his share of the loan, nor can the loan come from the sponsor of the project.

If all this sounds as if there's got to be a catch, you're right. In later years, when the wells are producing a pulsing stream of oil (or gas) to ease the nation's energy crisis, a high proportion of the revenue will go to pay off the indebtedness but will be credited to the income account of the investor. Thus, he will find himself paying taxes on income he doesn't actually receive. Nevertheless, it's still very much worthwhile, because that income, as well as the revenue he does receive, is subject to the 22 percent depletion allowance (up to a limit of 50 percent of net income). As a rule of thumb, about 30 percent of his cash income from the project should be tax-free to the investor because of the depletion allowance and deductions for operating expenses. Also, if the investor has paid for pipe and pumping equipment, his tax liability will be reduced by depreciation write-offs on it.

Timing of investments in oil and gas programs is important. True, they can be made as late as November and deductions of up to 100 percent may still be taken for that year. A sponsor may pay drilling costs late in the year and take deductions that year, even though the actual drilling doesn't take place until the following year. However, if the investor hopes to participate in a leveraged program, with deductions in excess of his input, the investment should be made by the end of summer.

Make sure you understand the amount of the first-year write-off. A New York broker several years ago invested $500,000 in a tax shelter under the impression that he would receive a 100 percent write-off and thus save $350,000 in taxes. On April 8 of the following year he found out that the write-off was only 60 percent and his tax saving was only $210,000. He had several days to find the additional $140,000 to meet his tax liability.

A provision of the tax law allows an individual who owns an interest in oil and gas properties to donate that interest to charity and take a tax deduction equal to its fair market value. If you're in a 60 percent tax bracket, this can be advantageous. Suppose you invest $10,000 in an oil and gas program which permits a 100 percent deduction in the first year, and it brings in wells worth $12,000. You already have a $6,000 tax saving; by donating your $12,000 interest to charity, you realize an additional tax saving of $7,200. Your profit on the arrangement is $3,200.

Sticking With Well-Established Operators

Oil and gas drilling programs got something of a bad name in the 1960's because of losses sustained by investors who went into deals with shoestring operators. Most of these have been weeded out by an IRS ruling that a corporate manager of a program must have a net worth of at least $250,000. Nevertheless, the professional man-investor usually will have a greater sense of security if he goes into a program managed by one of the big oil companies or one of about a dozen well-established independents with "track records" indicating they know their business.

Such operators are not difficult to find. McCulloch, one of the largest, has managed no less than thirty programs since 1956, into which investors have poured more than $100 million. If an investor had put $10,000 into each of the McCulloch programs through 1969, his after-tax cost would have been $185,362; by March 31, 1971, his share of producing wells would have been worth $890,870. Woods Corp., by mid-1971, had operated ten programs into which participants invested $34.4 million; besides tax benefits, they received back $12.1 million and the returns were still mounting. Apache Corp. has organized 31 programs with total subscriptions of $76.4 million; so far, investors have received $65.8 million in profits.

Which Professional Men Should Make Use of Tax-Sheltered Investments

Tax-sheltered investments, of course, are not for everyone. Unless, on a joint return, you have taxable income of $44,000 or more annually, which means you're in the 50 percent bracket, they are hardly worthwhile. As far as the professional man is concerned, the most significant aspect of the 1969 Tax Reform Act was that, for years after 1971, it set a maximum tax rate of 50 percent on earned income—salaries, professional fees, etc. For people who previously had been contributing a much higher proportion of their earned income to the support of the government, the search for tax sheltered investments thus has become somewhat less frantic. However, since the tax ceiling does not apply to income from other sources—rents, interest and dividends, for example—many professional men will find themselves in much higher tax brackets. Even without outside income, state and city income taxes will boost their effective bracket to 60 percent.

The Tax Reform Act also boosted from 25 percent to 35 percent the tax on capital gains of more than $50,000 realized in any one year. This made it important to find tax shelters for large capital gains as well as for some portion of the individual's regular income. Finally, the act imposed a 10 percent minimum tax on so-called "tax preference items" in excess of $30,000—a measure designed to prevent very wealthy persons from sheltering all of their income against taxes.

Once a decision has been made to seek out tax-sheltered investments, the next question is that of suitability. The shelter should be habitable. Here, it is important to realize that most tax-sheltered investments can't be easily liquidated if you should find yourself in a money pinch. A sufficient level of liquid assets—readily convertible into cash—should be maintained. One way to determine whether your reserves are adequate is to apply the sleep test. Ask yourself, "Could I sleep well knowing I had just invested $20,000 in a herd of cattle?"

The most extreme example of unsuitability your authors have run across was the sale of a $10,000 real estate partnership to a salesman with a salary of $8,000 a year. By taking a second mortgage on his house and selling what few stocks he owned, he was able to raise the $10,000. As soon as the brokerage house found out about the case, it quickly refunded the money. The salesman is now selling automobiles on the West Coast.

Most tax-shelter programs call for an initial investment of $5,000 or more, although in some states the minimum input is set at $10,000. Some swinging investors borrow all or some portion of the money from banks on some sort of short-term credit arrangement, repaying the loan when tax savings are realized. Programs which are sold through brokers and therefore have to be registered with the Securities and Exchange Commission must be paid for on the spot; anyone going into a private program which is not registered with the SEC should be very sure he is able to check out the sponsor's background and financial standing.

It is not uncommon for a program sponsor or manager to have the option of requesting additional funds from investors at some future time. Oil and gas drilling programs may be set up that way in order to ensure financing for the drilling of additional wells. In real estate programs, additional funds may be sought if rental income is not sufficient to cover debt servicing and the cost of maintaining the property. Investors should always read the fine print in any program prospectus to determine what further calls for funds may be made upon them, and what the tax consequences of additional investments will be.

One individual in Houston with an average annual income of about $50,000 had an unusual year recently, earning $250,000. He invested this entire amount in an oil venture. Much to his surprise, he received an assessment the following year for an additional $150,000. He had not even considered the possibility of additional funds being required by the promoter.

Joint Ventures and Limited Partnerships

Tax sheltered investment programs are organized either as joint ventures or as limited partnerships, the latter being the most common. Joint ventures are dangerous because of the unlimited liability of the participants; an investor could find himself embroiled in a suit for damages as a result of an employee's mistake and, if other participants were insolvent, might have to pay the entire bill himself. As a practical matter, of course, the program sponsor should carry insurance against any such eventuality, but it's still better to steer clear of joint ventures. A limited partnership, by contrast, is like a corporation in that each owner's liability is limited to the amount of his investment. In such an organization, however, there are limited partners and general partners; the latter, being management, are fully liable. Investors should beware of assuming any kind of management role in the firm without securing proper protection.

The reason for organizing a limited partnership rather than a corporation is that a partnership pays no taxes; the partners report their share of gains or losses on their own individual tax returns. Hence, deductions flow through to the individual and serve to reduce his taxable income. The partnership must be recognized as such by the Internal Revenue Service, and when tax-shelter programs are set up the normal procedure is to obtain such recognition from the IRS in advance, before any operations are begun. The general partner may be a corporation, but if that's the case the IRS will scrutinize the relationship to be sure it has sufficient capital and that no more than 20 percent of its stock is owned by the limited partners.

It is not only the IRS that should be interested in the financial responsibility of the general partner; limited partners should take a close, hard look themselves. In programs registered with the SEC, the prospectus will provide information on that subject, but in private offerings investors should insist on seeing an audited financial statement and make their own determination as to whether the sponsor is capable of fulfilling all his obligations. Those obligations may be pretty heavy. In an oil and gas program, for example, the general partner frequently undertakes to supply all the pumps, pipes and other depreciable equipment, and in a cattle breeding program it may be up to him to finance acquisition of the cattle.

Ordinarily, people who are in the business of sponsoring tax-sheltered investment programs make a part of their profit by supplying services to the program. The extent to which they plan to do so and the estimated costs usually will be set forth in the prospectus, and the investor will do well to compare several programs as to such costs before making a decision to put money into one of them. He should also see that the general partner employs a reputable accounting firm and a tax counsel which is knowledgeable regarding the type of venture to be launched.

Care should be taken, of course, to see that management fees are not out of line. Usually, there will be an initial charge which includes the sales commission of the underwriter, probably 8 percent of the investor's commitment, plus another 4 percent or so for legal fees, printing and other costs of the offering. In some programs the initial charge will also include an item for overhead costs of the sponsor, which may go as high as 10 percent. Then comes the continuing management fee, which may take any one of a number of different forms. A common arrangement is for the sponsor to take a percentage of the program's profits, after all expenses have been paid, or he may simply base his fee on the amount of money expended by the program. It should be noted that the best programs are not always those in which the management fees are lowest. In the final analysis, it's usually best to go with the sponsor who has a record of generating profits.

Drawback: Lack of Liquidity

As noted earlier, one of the chief drawbacks to tax-sheltered investments is that they lack liquidity. You can't call your broker and order him to sell at the market and, five days later, receive a check for the proceeds. In fact, one of the conditions for qualifying as a partnership is that the units are not freely transferable. Even if a sale is possible and a buyer can be found, the price will probably be far below the real worth of the asset. Nor is it possible to collateralize an interest in a program for purposes of obtaining a loan.

Some program sponsors do, however, provide some degree of liquidity for investors several years after the program has gotten under way. One method is simply for the sponsor to buy out the limited partners at a price based on anticipated future income. Another way is for the sponsor to offer shares of his stock in exchange for the program units. At that point, all income tax benefits of the program will have been exhausted, and the only consideration is the company's ability to operate the properties profitably and to conduct future programs successfully. Nevertheless, some stock exchange deals in the past have proved highly beneficial for the general partners. Participants in the 1968 oil drilling program of Adobe Corp., for example, were given the opportunity in 1970 of exchanging each $5,000 unit for 1,107 common shares of Adobe. Two years later, those shares were worth over $12,000.

QUESTIONS AND ANSWERS

Q. Why shouldn't a conservative investor in the 50%-or-above income tax bracket place all of his investment funds in municipal bonds? During the past 20 or more years, the various common stock averages have appreciated about 9% annually, and only 5% in the past three years, before income taxes and including reinvestment of all dividends. I have little faith that common stocks will do even this well in coming years. High-grade long-term municipal bonds now return about 6% tax-free, with maximum safety if held to maturity, and with a return that is equal to or exceeds the after-tax gain from common stocks.

From the sale of a successful side-line business, I am anticipating a net profit of $500,000, and am considering putting it all in municipals. What is your advice on this investment program, and what is the best way to make this purchase?

A. I believe you have greatly underestimated the possibilities of capital gains in well-chosen common stock. If you are knowledgeable, you can certainly beat the averages. Just two years ago, I bought American District Telegraph, a very conservative investment, at 23. It is now 48. That's over 100% in two years.

What I'm trying to illustrate is that you can do far better in stocks than in bonds. Of course, if your timing is off, you can lose a lot—in stocks and also in bonds. If you had bought tax-exempt bonds ten years ago, they would currently be worth less than what you paid for them. And the cash you would get if you sold them would buy less than two-thirds the amount of groceries it would have bought ten years ago.

Lesson number one in the kindergarten of investing is not to put all your eggs in one basket. If you are going to be faced with the problem of investing $500,000 shortly (we should all have such problems!) you would be well-advised to think in terms of (1) tax-exempt bonds or tax-exempt bond funds, (2) common stocks or common stock funds, and (3) convertible bonds or convertible preferred stocks.

15

THE PROFESSIONAL MAN'S KEOGH PLAN

Besides paying into the government's woefully inadequate Old Age Security plan, there are a number of ways for a corporation to provide for the declining years of employees and executives, using tax-free dollars. Funds allocated to pension and profit-sharing programs escape the clutches of the Internal Revenue Service—at least until the beneficiary retires. But until recently the only way for professional men and other self-employed people to enjoy the same privilege was to set up personal corporations, a complex and expensive procedure which immediately stamped them as tax evaders. To give such people a break, Congress finally passed legislation permitting so-called Keogh plans, named after Rep. Eugene Keogh, Dem., of Brooklyn. His original bill, passed in 1962, placed so many restrictions on the pension programs it envisaged that few self-employed people thought it was worth the bother, but liberalizing amendments were passed in 1968, and a bill to broaden it further was introduced in 1972.

The Basic Concept of the Keogh Amendment

The Keogh amendment to the Internal Revenue Act is infernally complicated in its various ramifications, but the concept is simple enough. If you're self-employed, you can set aside 10 percent of your income, but not more than $2,500 per year, in a pension fund, paying no federal income tax on it. You invest the money, one way or another, and the yield from the investment, being plowed back into the fund, is also tax-free. Only when you retire is the money subject to income taxes, but at that point you'll be in a much lower tax bracket and the bite will be less painful.

Under the 1972 amendment, the amount which could be paid into a Keogh plan each year was to be raised to 15 percent of the contributor's income, not to exceed $7,000 annually.

If the self-employed person has any employees—salaried nurses, secretaries, etc.— he must set up Keogh pension plans for them, too, of which more anon. In that case, he can make an additional "voluntary contribution" of up to $2,500 (or $7,000 under the 1972 amendment) to his own pension fund. Regular income taxes must be paid on that amount, but the yield that results from investing it is tax-free. After retirement, of course, the taxes that were paid on the voluntary contributions can be deducted from whatever liability is incurred through withdrawals from the fund.

Using tax-free dollars to build up a pension fund is a great advantage. If one were to save on that basis, say, $1,000 annually for twenty years, drawing 4 percent on the money, at the end of two decades the fund would have $29,778 in it. On the other hand, assume that the contributor is in a 50 percent tax bracket and is trying to build up a pension fund without benefit of a Keogh plan. To start with, if he were to devote the same proportion of his net income to the effort, he would be able to pay in only $500 a year. Then, in effect, he'd only be receiving 2 percent interest on the money, since the tax collector would be grabbing the other 2 percent. After two decades the fund would contain only $11,910. The difference between that figure and $29,778 is what the Keogh plan is worth to a professional man in such circumstances—$17,868.

Obviously, Keogh plans are very much worthwhile for the self-employed—professional men as well as small businessmen, writers, inventors, entertainers and professional athletes. All such people are eligible. Nor is there any age limit; you can start a Keogh plan the year before you plan to retire if you like, sheltering from taxes 10 percent of that year's income, or $2,500, whichever is less.

Employees Also Benefit

To be sure, there are some drawbacks. The most important one is that, if you have any employees that are connected with the business that is supporting the pension fund, you must set up a Keogh plan for them, too. If you're a doctor, dentist or lawyer, for example, that would mean any full-time office nurse, clerk or secretary who is on a salary. It would not apply, however, to domestic help in your home, or to part-time and seasonal workers—the nurse you hire for a month while the other girl is on vacation.

Calling this aspect of Keogh plans a drawback depends entirely on your point of view; there are professional men who welcome the chance to provide greater security for nurses and office workers, who may be trusted, loyal employees deserving of every consideration. In such cases, it is a great advantage to be able to provide for them with tax-free dollars. Sentimental considerations aside, a generous pension scheme will help you to keep valuable employees, who might otherwise be tempted to find jobs with corporations that do offer pension plans.

What it amounts to is that, if you are contributing, say, 10 percent of your earned income to a Keogh-type pension plan for yourself, then you must finance a plan for each employee equal to 10 percent of his or her salary. Thus, suppose you're a doctor whose practice, after deducting all costs, yields $30,000 a year of earned income. In setting up a Keogh plan, you decide to take the maximum write-off for yourself, which in this case (assuming that the 1972 amendment allowing a $7,000 maximum didn't pass) will be $2,500. That works out to 8.33 percent of your net earned income. But you have an office nurse whom you pay $8,000 a year. You must, then, set up a Keogh plan for her into which you will pay 8.33 percent of her salary, or $666.40. However, since the contribution is a pre-tax expense, the real cost to you is only $493. It should be remembered that, once assumed, this obligation is constant, as long as the nurse remains in your service and you continue to make contributions into your own Keogh pension plan. If she quits, or leaves your employ for any reason at all, the amount accumulated in her pension fund is hers and must be paid to her on her departure. However, no Keogh plan fund need be established for her successor until the new nurse has been with you for three years. (The 1972 amendment changes this to two years if the employee is between 30 and 35 years of age, or one year if she is over 35.) Two doctors sharing the same receptionist, incidentally, cannot deny her the benefit of a Keogh plan on the ground that she is working only part-time for each; they must contribute to her plan in the same proportion as they are contributing to their own.

There are ways to reduce the burden of employee Keogh plans. You can, for example, set up a "benefit-oriented" plan. Assume, for the sake of argument, a case where a consulting engineer earns an annual income of $50,000 and has a secretary to whom he pays $6,000 per year. If he sets up a Keogh plan into which he pays the maximum $2,500 per year for himself, or 5 percent of his income, he would normally have to pay $300 per year into a fund for the secretary—5 percent of her annual salary. Under a benefit-oriented plan, he would, with his $2,500 a year, buy an insurance annuity which, on retirement, would pay him a monthly income of $425. That would be 10.22 percent of his annual salary. Therefore, he can arrange a pension plan which, on retirement, will pay the secretary 10.22 percent of her salary, or $51 per month. She is only 23 years old, so the cost of setting up such an annuity would be only about $110 per year.

Another way is to adopt the profit-sharing approach, where contributions are made into Keogh plan pension funds only above a certain level of earnings. Thus, if the business earns $35,000 a year and the fixed minimum you have set is $15,000, you can contribute 10 percent of the remainder, or $2,000, into your own pension fund. But the $2,000 is only 5.6 percent of the total earnings of $35,000, so you need contribute only 5.6 percent of each employee's annual salary to his fund. Also, the law permits pension plans to be "integrated" with social security, which in effect means that the employer's contribution to each worker's pension fund can be lessened by the amount he pays in social security taxes for that employee; various limitations on this method, however, make it applicable only where a sizable number of employees are involved.

What to Do With the Money

Once you're committed to a Keogh plan, it's irrevocable. You can't take the money out—you can't even borrow against it—until the day you retire. Moreover, the government requires that some method of funding be established which, up to a point, places the money beyond your control. One thing you can do, as noted earlier, is buy an annuity from an insurance company, either of the fixed or variable type. In the former case, you pay in so much money; when you either retire or die, you or your survivors will get either a lump sum or a specified income each month—usually the latter. If you buy the variable annuity, by contrast, the amount of money you get back depends on how successful the insurance company is in its investments. Insurance companies have had trouble selling endowment policies because the public, after thirty years of experience, has come to the realization that they are not viable in an inflationary economy. In a variable annuity program, presumably, there is a built-in hedge against inflation because the company's investment yield will grow in proportion to the decline in the value of the money. It may not work, but it's a nice theory.

You can also put the money into a mutual fund, via "face amount certificates," which are non-transferable. That satisfies the government requirement that you keep your hands off the money. Still another way is to buy Government Retirement Bonds on a regular basis, or you can hand it over to a bank to invest as it sees fit, under a custodial arrangement. Finally, you can set up a trust fund, administered by a bank or trust company. The latter is the most expensive arrangement—it costs one half of one percent of the amount of money in the fund each year—but it also is the most flexible. The trust can be set up any way you like, and you can arrange it so that you direct the investments. If you're reading this book, it's probably because you want to handle the investment of your own money; hence, you probably will want to administer your own Keogh plan. You can do so under a trust fund arrangement.

One point that should be stressed is that, in a Keogh plan, you're dealing with tax-free money. Therefore, you don't have to worry about whether any capital gains are short-term or long-term. It doesn't matter. And normally short-term gains are a lot easier to realize than those of the long-term variety.

The advantage of being able to take short-term profits is illustrated by the case of a West Coast physician who established a Keogh plan in 1968 as a means of funding his speculations in the new issue market. He set it up as a self-administered trust and contributed to it the maximum $5,000—$2,500 in voluntary contributions and a like amount in ordinary input. Stock market buffs will recall that 1968 was the biggest year in history for new stock issues, many of which went to fantastic premiums as soon as they were floated. The doctor played that game for all it was worth, and during the year he made over 1,000 trades, buying and selling just-issued stocks with his $5,000 fund. Well, actually, after the first few trades he had more than that to play with, because he made money on them. And twelve months after he first established his pension fund it contained a little over $180,000. Since the money was in his Keogh plan pension fund, he had no taxes to pay on the capital gain.

Getting Your Money Out Later

At least, he had no taxes to pay until he reached retirement age. And that brings us to the last act of the Keogh drama—how to get your money out with a minimum tax payment. It doesn't make much sense, after all, to accumulate, say, $100,000 in a pension fund if, in the year that you decide to retire, the government takes $45,000 of it. To avoid that, you must set the plan up right in the beginning, making it as flexible as possible. See that the rules under which your Keogh plan is established provide for the following kinds of distribution: (1) lump sum; (2) retirement plan government bonds; (3) systematic withdrawals; (4) annuities, either guaranteed or variable.

Thus, you leave all options open for the day you finally decide to go into retirement, since who knows what the tax structure will be at that time? Incidentally, as the rules stand now, you cannot touch the money in your Keogh plan fund until you are 59½ years of age, and you must do so no later than the tax year in which you reach 70½. Most people, of course, will want to take out the money in whatever way results in the smallest tax bite.

The best way, generally, is to buy some kind of annuity. Or rather, for the form, you don't buy it, the trustee of the fund buys it for you. Thus, you have never received money from the fund and, as the Internal Revenue Service puts it, no "taxable event" has occurred. The only money you receive is your monthly payout from the annuity. On that, you must pay income taxes at the ordinary rate, but since you now are retired and presumably have a much lower income, the damage won't be too great.

There are ways to cut it down. For one thing, you don't have to pay taxes again on your voluntary contributions to the fund, and if you wish to do so you can take advantage of the "cost-recovery-first" provision as far as they are concerned. The idea here is that all your costs of setting up an annuity can be recovered in the early years of the annuity—precisely, the first three years—without your having to pay any tax on them. The voluntary contributions are considered part of that cost. Also, if you are over 65 at the time of your retirement, you can take advantage of the retirement income credit. The maximum credit is $1,524, to which a rate of 15 percent is applied, thus reducing your tax liability by up to $228.60.

Insurance companies will provide all the information you want, and more, on the various types of annuity programs available. Some Keogh plan contributors, however, may not wish to retire when they are 70½. If you should elect to stay in harness a few years longer, being forced to set up your annuity program at that age would be a hardship, since the benefits will be added to your regular income, increasing your tax liability proportionately, at a time when you don't really need the money. The way around that is to have the trustee of your Keogh fund buy government retirement bonds. Again, when he does so, no taxable event occurs. You can hold off cashing the bonds, which meanwhile yield 4½ percent, until you do retire.

Under some circumstances, it may be desirable to take all or part of your Keogh plan funds in a lump sum. While the amount is taxable at the ordinary income rate, there are some possibilities for reducing the liability. To start with, once again, you need not pay taxes on any amounts paid into the fund as voluntary contributions, and half of any funds paid prior to 1968 are in the same category. The tax on the remainder can be figured by a system of lump-sum averaging. Say, for example, you're withdrawing $15,000 from the fund in a year when earnings from other sources amount to $7,000. You add one-fifth of the amount withdrawn, or $3,000, to your regular income, and then take your normal deductions, which might amount to, say, $2,500. Compute your tax on that amount, probably around $1,600. Now, figure your tax on your $7,000 of regular income minus the $3,000—or $4,000. It will amount to about $900. Finally, take the difference between the $1,600 and the $900 (or $700) and multiply it by five—$3,500. That is your tax liability on the $15,000 withdrawal from the fund.

Professional men who want to go more deeply into the tax and investment aspects of Keogh plans should read a book written by a friend and colleague of ours, Steven S. Anreder. Entitled *Retirement Dollars for the Self-Employed,* it is published by Thomas Y. Crowell Co., New York, N.Y.

QUESTIONS AND ANSWERS

Q. I have been investing my Keogh Plan money in the Dreyfus Fund but feel that it is unwise to put all the eggs in one basket. I would like to diversify by investing the Keogh money in several funds. Is this possible? Is it also possible to pull the money out of a fund, if I wish?

A. As a physician in private practice, you may invest in two or more funds under Keogh. If you make your investments directly, rather than through a special trust fund, your right to pull your money out of one fund and put it into another will depend on the restrictions imposed, if any, by the first fund's plan. Some funds require the money to ride until taken as income in retirement; others permit the money to be transferred to another mutual fund. So it is important to read the small print in the brochure before choosing your Keogh mutual fund.

A special trust can provide you, through your trustee, the flexibility of investing in whichever funds you like (regardless of their attitude on restricting the movement of your investment dollars)—and perhaps in real estate, commodities, and other investment media. The trust officer at your bank may have a standard Keogh trust arrangement for you, although many banks long since have given up handling Keogh plans, as they apparently prove more trouble than they are worth.

16

SETTING UP A PROFESSIONAL CORPORATION

Professional men whose income is sufficiently high to enable them to pour much more money into a retirement fund than the $2,500 per year permissible under a Keogh plan ($7,000 if the 1972 amendment goes through), may wish to adopt the alternative of setting up a professional corporation. When that is done, there is no dollar limit on the amount that can be set aside. Using a combination of pension and profit sharing plans, it is possible to stash away as much as 25 percent of income in a tax-deductible retirement fund.

If you have a Keogh plan in operation and want to go the professional corporation route, it is now possible to transfer the assets from your Keogh fund to your corporation pension fund without penalty. Until a few years ago that was not practical because the Internal Revenue Service insisted that it amounted to a premature distribution of the Keogh plan assets; hence, the beneficiary would have to pay taxes on the entire amount immediately. The T-men have relented on that score, but it is still wise to keep a separate account of the Keogh plan money, in case you decide to retire before the age of 59½. Remember that it cannot be distributed earlier without running into thorny tax questions. The thing to do if you've had enough of the rat race at, say, age 55, is to draw on the retirement fund of your professional corporation, leaving the Keogh plan fund intact for another four-and-a-half years.

First, Look at the Drawbacks

There are some disadvantages in setting up a professional corporation which you should certainly consider before taking the plunge.

One is that it can be expensive. Costs vary from state to state, so it's impractical to give any accurate estimate here, but your attorney can give you a quick run-down. There will be filing fees, some printing costs, a lot of legal work. Unless you're able to put aside for retirement substantially more than the sums allowed under a Keogh plan, it won't be worthwhile.

It's also a nuisance. In order to enjoy the tax benefits of a corporate form, you must actually operate a real corporation. The IRS takes a dim view of phony ones, obvious tax loopholes. This means holding regular meetings of the board of directors, keeping minutes of the meetings, actually voting on all proposals. The red tape involved in making your little fiction look credible can be burdensome.

There is no little risk that the IRS one day will move decisively against professional corporations. While the government does recognize that the self-employed have as much right to provide for their old age as salaried people or corporate executives, the Keogh program has been set up for them and is considered by Treasury people as the appropriate vehicle. Until 1969, the IRS refused to recognize professional corporations at all, and it was only after a series of court cases were decided against it that the agency gave in; it still doesn't like them. It's likely that eventually the IRS, in its recommendations to Congress, will accept broad liberalization of the Keogh program in return for an end to professional corporations.

Meanwhile, there is a danger that your little one-man corporation might be designated a personal holding company—the ultimate disaster. Accumulations of income by personal holding companies are taxed at a whopping 70 percent. And what's the difference between a professional corporation and a personal holding company? It's a fine line. The former, like General Motors, is a stockholder concern run by a board of directors which designates officers, who, in turn, tell all the employees what to do. A personal holding company is one where a single individual holds 25 percent or more of the stock, where the same individual performs all or most of the services rendered by the company, and where that individual effectively makes the corporate decisions. It's easy to see how the IRS, in its greed, might mistake a professional corporation for a personal holding company.

To guard against any such error on the part of the IRS, some experts on professional corporations recommend that they take vows of poverty, like priests. All their income, after expenses, should be paid out, either as salary or in the form of dividends, and they should not hold any appreciable amount of property. Some professional men who have incorporated themselves even go to such lengths as leasing their office furniture, along with all technical equipment, to make sure the company has no assets which could be construed as hiding places for income. The idea is that, if there are no assets, the IRS won't think you are squirreling away some of your revenue in the recesses of the company rather than reporting it out as income, where it can be taxed.

There are still a couple of minor drawbacks to be considered. One is that the cost of social security coverage under a corporate setup is considerably higher than for an individual owner-employer. Another is that, if you have any employees, they become immediately eligible for inclusion in your corporate pension plan; there can be no three-year waiting period, as in a Keogh plan.

Look on the Bright Side

On the other hand, the professional corporation formula offers some significant advantages, in addition to its greater pension plan potential.

One is that, if a monetary emergency should strike, you can borrow money from your own pension fund. Keogh doesn't permit that. Of course, it must be a bona fide loan, at competitive rates of interest.

Another is that, if you like, you can retire as early as age 50 and start withdrawing benefits from your pension plan, whereas the Keogh plan forces you to wait until you're 59½.

If you should die, your heirs will qualify for exclusion from estate taxes on the benefits of a corporate pension fund. Under a Keogh plan they do not.

A corporation can provide its employees—including you as the owner-employee—with health and disability insurance, as well as group life insurance up to $50,000, deducting the premiums from pre-tax income as a business expense. On the life insurance, it can go higher than $50,000, but then the employee must pay a small tax on the excess premium.

Under some circumstances, setting up a corporation may also ease the tax bite. The reason is that small companies with net income of less than $25,000 pay taxes at the rate of 22 percent. (Above that amount, however, the levy jumps to 48 percent.) Suppose, for instance, you're a dentist with a taxable income of $50,000. As an individual (married, filing a joint return), your tax on that amount of income is $14,060 plus 50 percent of the excess over $44,000, for a total of $17,060. However, if you're technically employed by a professional corporation you can plow the excess over $44,000—the $6,000—back into the company. Assuming that the firm doesn't have net income of more than $25,000, it will pay taxes on the $6,000 only at the rate of 22 percent, or $1,320. You save $1,680. Of course, the $6,000 must be employed in some worthwhile corporate endeavor; otherwise—remember the punitive rates on personal holding companies?

Bigger and Better Pension Plans

The main advantage of a professional corporation, however, is that you can stash away more tax-free money in a retirement fund. Remember that under a Keogh plan, unless the liberalizing 1972 amendment is passed by Congress, the maximum contribution you can make to your retirement fund each year is 10 percent of your income or $2,500, whichever is less. A maximum of another $2,500 can be added to the fund annually, which isn't tax-free; the yield or capital gains it generates, however, isn't taxed until you retire. Under a corporate setup, in contrast, you can set up a profit-sharing plan in which 15 percent of net profits goes into a fund for employees—including yourself. However, if a so-called "money purchase" plan is used, the upper limit is 10 percent. That takes a little explaining. Generally, if you go to an insurance company and say you want to buy an annuity, they'll say, "For how much?" You set a figure, like $100,000, and they'll tell you how much you must pay in every year, for how many years, to reach that total. Under a money purchase plan, however, you don't specify how much you're going to get out, but how much you're able to put in this year, say $5,000. Next year business may be poor, so you only contribute $2,000, but the following year $7,000. The amounts that you contribute can be as variable as you like, and so will be the payout. The latter is worked out on an actuarial basis, taking into account the input of funds and the number of years the insurer has the use of your money. Money purchase plans are extensively used in retirement plans set up by professional corporations.

Along with the company's profit-sharing plan, it can also have a pension plan, in which the benefits are related to the employee's salary and length of service. Some corporations with elderly employees get away with pension plan contributions as high as 40 percent or 50 percent of the employees' salaries. However, if there's a combination pension fund and profit-sharing fund, about the most you can put into it is 25 percent of the company's net income.

Case History of a Doctor Who Incorporated

Insurance companies, on the lookout for annuity premiums, put out packaged plans for professional corporations, as they do Keogh plans. One of these plans shows the advantage, from a tax-saving standpoint, over unincorporated status, for a fifty-year-old doctor whose gross income is $80,000 per year.

As postulated, the subject has been in private practice for twenty years, has no retirement plan at all, but has assets of approximately $200,000, plus life insurance of $200,000. He employs a full-time nurse at an annual salary of $7,800. The assets are shown as $10,000 in cash, a $75,000 residence (owned by his wife), $15,000 worth of office furnishings and equipment, and $100,000 in securities.

Other assumptions: The doctor's office overhead, besides wages, amounts to $14,200. Income from his personal investments is $4,000 per year. The annual premiums on his life insurance are $3,600, and he spends another $1,000 per year for disability insurance which, if he were to be disabled, would pay him a monthly income of $2,000. He has two children in college, at an annual cost of $8,000. Altogether, his living costs total $37,000 a year, and his income tax statement shows deductions of $8,000 for interest, property taxes, contributions, etc.

Under the plan set up for him, the doctor's professional corporation would pay him an annual salary of $43,200, as compared to the $56,000 he has been taking out of his practice. Note, however, that his taxes are $6,100 less per year. Instead of the $6,700 now left over for investment, he is putting $10,800 into his pension and profit-sharing plans. Another $2,000 is contributed to a pension and profit-sharing program for his nurse. Figure 16-1 shows the detailed figures.

Now let's look at the results fifteen years later, when the doctor is ready to retire. Had he continued to operate as an unincorporated professional, putting away $6,700 a year in investments, he'd now have $168,170 available for retirement, assuming an annual yield of 7 percent from his investments. However, since he would have to pay income taxes each year on that yield, the investment would compound at a rate of only 4 percent.

By way of contrast, under the corporate plan, the doctor would be socking away $10,800 per year in his profit-sharing and pension plans. At the same 7 percent rate

	Unincorporated Professional		Incorporated Professional	
Gross Revenue Practice		$80,000		$80,000
Cost of Operations				
Employees Wages	$ 8,000		$ 8,000	
Professionals Salary	—		43,200	
Other Overhead	16,000		16,000	
Pension and Profit-Sharing				
Employee	—		2,000	
Stockholder	—		10,800	
Total		24,000		80,000
Earned Income/Corp. Profit		$56,000		None
Practitioners Income				
Earned Income/Salary		56,000		43,200
Investment Income		4,000		4,000
Total Income		$60,000		$47,200
Itemized Deductions	8,000		8,000	
Personal Exemption	3,000		3,000	
Taxable	$11,000		$11,000	
Tax				
Federal	$13,800		8,400	
State	5,500	19,300	4,800	13,200
Net Income After Taxes		40,700		34,000
Add Back Exemptions		3,000		3,000
		$43,700		$37,000
Deduct Cost of Living		37,000		37,000
Net for Investments		$ 6,700		–0–

of yield, the retirement fund at the end of fifteen years would contain $271,080. Assuming a lump sum distribution at that time, taxes on the accumulation would be $63,880, providing distribution takes place in the year the doctor left practice and he had no other earned income. Thus, the net funds available to him would be $207,200, or almost 24 percent more than if he had gone his way unincorporated.

The insurance company says that is conservative; by rule of thumb, a professional corporation should do 26 percent better. Moreover, because of the provision excluding the proceeds of a pension or profit-sharing plan from estate taxes, the doctor's heirs, if he should die at about retirement age, would get $58,485 more because of the professional corporation plan.

QUESTIONS AND ANSWERS

Q. I am a 35-year-old married physician. I incorporated a year ago and am ready to invest $10,000 in a pension and profit-sharing plan. I would appreciate your advice on what to invest in—stocks, bonds, real estate, mutual funds, oil ventures?

A. If the fund does not have to pay a tax on its income, you might consider picking out half a dozen or so high-yield convertible bonds or convertible preferred stocks, where there are both good current income and the chance of long-term capital appreciation. Harbor Fund is a mutual fund whose primary activity is in convertibles.

Q. If, as you have mentioned, pension funds do not have to pay any annual income taxes on short-term gains, I could be much more aggressive in managing our pension fund than could most mutual funds, couldn't I?

A. No doubt you could. But, playing the market for short-term profits is a nervous business, and your practice could suffer. Some doctors say that while the odds may favor the day trader, they are definitely against his patients.

17

HOW A SHORT SELLER TAKES HIS PROFITS

Mr. M.B., Wall Street's "Black Prince of Bad Stocks," got interested in a stock called Acme Missiles while doing his "homework" in the public reading room of the Securities and Exchange Commission. There he noticed, in a routine monthly report called an 8-K form, that an insurance company had cancelled Acme Missile's construction bond. That little bit of information sent waves of delight down his plump physique.

"The bond cancellation meant the company's credit had gone sour, so I shorted the stock," M.B. explains. The stock was selling at 30 when he shorted it.

Four days later, as the story got around, the stock dropped to 15. Then it rallied back up to 25, and M.B. and his customers (a coterie of professional portfolio managers and wealthy individuals) shorted the stock some more. The stock gradually declined again, and dropped very sharply a few weeks later when the American Stock Exchange announced it was investigating the company's affairs.

M.B. still held on to his short position, because his own investigations of the company had convinced him by this time that it would soon be delisted and perhaps go bankrupt. After the delisting, to make a long story short, M.B. and his customers covered their short positions at less than 2, making almost 100 percent on their money.

The incident was really just another example of how much money can be made in the stock market by people who are willing to take the trouble to do their "homework."

Finding the Phonies

M.B.'s specialty was finding stocks that were "phonies" and taking a big short position in them for himself and his clients. A short seller sells stock he does not have, and then buys it back at a lower price (if he is successful), thus realizing a profit. Most short sellers are not successful. They end up buying the stock back at a higher price instead of a lower price. Some traders have been completely wiped out by selling the wrong stocks short at the wrong time. There is no limit to how much you can lose if a stock you sold short keeps going up. Hence the old saw, "He who sells what isn't his'n/ Buys it back or goes to prison."

For most investors, especially for busy professional men, selling short is just a bad bet. The most you can win (if the company vanishes and the stock drops to zero) is 100 percent, and the gains are all short-term gains, fully taxable. But there is no limit to how much you can lose. It is much better to buy stocks that will go up. That way there is no limit to how much you might win, and if the company is basic to the U.S. economy and the price-earnings ratio is low, you usually can't lose very much.

M.B. is a rarity among brokers in that he has made most of his fortune, for himself and his customers, by shorting stocks. The stocks he shorted were stocks that had been pushed way up in price despite the fact that they were essentially worthless or worth very little. The history of the stock market is replete with examples of stocks that one way or another get pushed up to prices far in excess of their intrinsic worth. It is also replete with examples of stocks that rise after a company announces a fantastic new product that, in reality, doesn't exist.

One day M.B., who has a nose for such situations, went to see the chairman of the executive committee of a company whose stock was listed on the American Stock Exchange, to learn more about a certain highly-publicized electronics device that the company would make public comments about whenever it wanted its stock to go higher. "I talked to this so-called electronics expert and the more I questioned him, the more I saw that he knew nothing about his company," said M.B. "Finally the guy admitted that he was a former butcher and didn't know beans about electronics or about the famous machine his company was getting ready to market—or any machine. That's when I decided to sell the stock short."

Another hunch led him to visit a small company that had become popular among traders because it was working on a new office copier. M.B. was greeted at the door by the director of research. "When this research director started demonstrating the machine to me, it was obvious that he didn't know how to work it." The next morning M.B. began building a large short position in the stock. The stock collapsed a few months later, and no one ever heard of the copier again.

The key ingredient here, of course, is taking the trouble to find out the facts. While other Wall Street analysts were willing to repeat what they read about the company's new products, M.B. went and saw for himself. Anyone who assumes the enormous risk of selling short must base the short sale on first-hand information. For the busy professional man, this rules out most short-selling.

"Most fund managers are shoemakers," M.B. is quoted as saying in the *Wall Street Journal*. "I'm not the world's most brilliant person, but the longer I'm in this business, the more jerks I see and the more convinced I am that most of the people in the stock market are sheep."

Needless to say, our friend M.B. is not the most popular man on Wall Street! But his basic negativity—evidenced in these few quotes—always came in handy when most investors were getting far too exuberant. M.B. says his parents wanted him to be a rabbi or a doctor. His father, in fact, was a rabbi. "That's why I'm very moral," he says, "and when I see worthless stocks going sky high, I get angry and want to sell them short."

Short Selling Is Nerve Wracking

Sometimes, even for M.B., it can be a devastating, nerve-wracking way to make a living. One of his first shorts was a company called Fotochrome, which claimed it was soon coming out with a color camera that would out-Polaroid Polaroid, and television tubes three inches thick. As the announcements kept reappearing regularly, although analysts who visited the company never saw the alleged new products, M.B. began to suspect the worst. So he and his customers began shorting the stock at $7. However, the stock kept going up, and M.B. got clobbered by it because he did not have enough money to hold out. (A short seller must deposit a percentage of the value of the stock he has sold short, in cash. As the price of the stock rises, the amount of cash he must deposit also rises.)

"I had to cover at $19, and I lost about $30,000, which was a lot of money to me back then. Three days later the stock hit a high of $20, and then broke. It fell to $1.88" (1⅞). Two of his clients stuck it out and made a killing, but a lot of smaller investors got hurt. Since then, M.B. has refused to handle short sales for small investors, and has specialized in handling them for hedge funds—mutual funds that have part of their portfolio in short positions.

What Not to Sell Short

The less experienced trader is usually tempted to sell short a stock that has been acting so strongly that it appears to be much too high. Such a short sale usually turns out to be a bear trap, for in the stock market, as we have noted again and again in foregoing chapters, stocks that are going strong usually tend to continue going strong. Often, in fact, these stocks attract so many short sellers that the short position becomes too crowded. There are too many shorts waiting frantically to cover their positions before they run out of cash and are forced to cover at a disastrous loss. Often they all get scared out of their short positions at once, pushing the stock sharply higher as they buy back the shares they sold short.

Before selling a stock short, you must always wait for the bubble to burst. Once it bursts the stock will go downward for a long time, and although you won't be able to take your short position right at the top, at least you will be able to take it with much less risk. M.B.'s success with Acme Missiles is only a slight exception to this rule. He happened to anticipate by a few days the bursting of the bubble when he saw the news of the bond cancellation. His experience with Fotochrome is a good example of what can happen if you short a stock that is still going strong and that the public is still excited about. Had he waited for the stock to start downward, using the technical approach to determine that a downtrend was now under way, he would have had ample opportunity to short the stock on brief rallies and come out way ahead.

A second category that short sellers should be careful to avoid is a company with a relatively small floating supply of stock. If the float is small, it is often possible for large stockholders to keep the stock up, or push it even higher, as explained in Chapter 2.

A short position in such a stock can become overcrowded very quickly, and in the process of covering their positions, the short sellers may be forced to bid the price up sharply. The companies with very heavy floating supplies of stock—that is, the highly liquid stocks—are the safest ones to sell short, if any short sale can correctly be called safe. And it is not enough to look at the total number of shares outstanding, because demand for the stock could still result in a relatively thin float. You have to examine the chart very carefully to see how "easily" the stock can go up. In other words, if a slight pick-up in trading volume makes the stock jump 2 or 3 points, don't sell it short. If an enormous increase in volume only raises the price a fraction of a point, the stock may be a short sale candidate.

Generally speaking, the short seller assumes somewhat less risk if he sticks to companies with at least four million shares outstanding or more. Often, of course, the best short possibilties exist in smaller companies. But you can only short these if you have uncovered the kind of solid, first-hand information that M.B. acted on.

Short Positions as a Hedge Against Long Positions

There are a number of large traders, including the hedge funds, that proceed on the theory that all their bets are at least partially hedged if they are long on stocks that they think are going up, and short on stocks that they think are going down. The usual balance is to have about 80 percent of the portfolio in long positions and about 20 percent in short positions. If the selections are good, the short positions will show gains during market declines, and the long positions will show gains during bull markets. If the selections are exceptionally well made, it is perfectly possible for both long and short positions to show gains at the same time. The main idea behind the hedged portfolio is that during a bad break at least some news will be good. The picture won't all be black— at least, so the theory goes. In practice, many of the big hedge funds have done worse than almost anyone else during bear market periods, but that was because they were poorly run, not because the approach was unsound.

QUESTIONS AND ANSWERS

Q. I own 500 A.T.&T. warrants at a cost of 6¾. Now my broker tells me that the reason they haven't done anything is that a lot of professionals have sold them short. If the pro's are selling them short, shouldn't I get out of them quickly?

A. Not necessarily, if your objective is long-term appreciation. These warrants expire in just a few years. Unless the common stock rises above 52 by that time, the warrants will become worthless on the expiration date. Can you see why the pro's are selling the warrants short and buying the common stock as a hedge? If the common does go above 52, the pro's will make on the common what they lose on the short sale of the warrants. If the common does not rise above 52, they will make 100 percent on their short sale. This is a hedged bet for them, the best way to sell short.

18

READING BETWEEN THE LINES OF THE FINANCIAL PAGES

Ask a newspaper man the question, "What is news?" and the chances are he'll tell you that news is what the editor says is news.

A lot of financial news comes straight from the public relations departments of publicly traded corporations, or from the treasurer, financial vice-president, or president of the corporation. These corporate officials decide what the news about their corporation should be. Then the financial editors of the various news media, in turn, decide which of the news items manufactured by corporate officials are to be printed and to become NEWS. In other words, the financial news you read comes off an assembly line of sorts, and there are many places along the line where it can be, and almost always is, molded, shaped, and tampered with so that it produces a desired effect.

The desired effect may be to make the stock go up or to make it go down. If the stock is already in an uptrend, and news is manufactured to make it go up still higher, the manufacturing process will succeed in making it go still higher. On the other hand, if the stock is in a well-entrenched downtrend, the same kind of news will only have a temporary effect. There will be a brief rally for a day or two, and then the news will be brushed aside and the downtrend will continue.

The Manipulation Cycle

One obvious way to manufacture news that will make a stock go up is to report higher earnings than most investors expected. The corporation's financial officers have quite a bit of leeway. If, for example, they want to report higher earnings than last year, but actual net operating revenues were less, they can make up the difference by slowing the rate at which they are depreciating their plant and equipment. This adds to earnings, although it also adds to taxes and therefore leaves the company with less cash for expansion or other purposes. The financial men can also add to earnings by deferring expenses that should really be kept in the expense column of the current year. And there are numerous other techniques for making reported earnings look better than they should, including tampering with inventories, capitalizing costs that should be expensed rather than capitalized, changing the manner in which the earnings of subsidiary companies are taken into the parent company's income statement, and so on. As you might expect, for every gimmick that raises reported earnings, there is a comparable gimmick for lowering reported earnings.

Why would corporate insiders want to lower reported earnings? Remember that the stock market is essentially a cyclical phenomenon. You can't always manipulate a stock upward. At some point you have to sell and then manipulate it downward so that you can buy it back at a lower price.

Typically, a "cycle of manipulation" would unfold in somewhat the following way: A stock has been going down for quite some time and is currently at least 50 percent below its most recent peak. The company has had a number of problems that have resulted in higher costs and therefore narrower profit margins. But now the insiders are eying their own stock again because of the low price. Furthermore, they see a big pickup ahead in sales within their industry, and realize that profit margins will widen again as sales increase, and the company will be able to report higher earnings than ever in about two years.

The first step, then, is to get the stock down even lower, so the insiders can buy it at bargain-basement levels. In a meeting of the executive and finance committee, two decisions are reached: First, the company will write off a sizable amount of inventory against current income, put millions of extra dollars into this year's research and development expenses, and take whatever other steps are available to lower net income this year and, at the same time, allow for a big increase in net income next year. The second decision is to convince the board of directors at the next dividend meeting to reduce the dividend "in order to conserve cash." This is the surest way to make the stock sell off. In fact, the officials also decided that they would allow the news of the impending dividend cut to leak out a little here and there, so that the stock would begin to sink well before the directors' meeting.

The directors meet, vote to cut the dividend, and the president issues a statement to the Dow Jones ticker tape reporter, emphasizing the negative aspects of the current outlook. The stock sells off sharply, and is now about 75 percent below its peak. Finally, the corporate insiders, others close to the company, and all their friends and relatives and what not, begin buying the stock, at a very low price, considering the prospects for improvement over the coming two or three years.

On the charts, a bottom, or base, is forming as those in the know continue buying. When they have completed their buying, the company suddenly becomes very optimistic about its prospects. Analysts from brokerage houses and advisory services are given a glowing account of how the company is turning the corner, revitalizing itself, and preparing to invade new markets with exciting new products and a greatly improved sales organization. These analysts, in turn, prepare bullish reports on the company, and the stock starts to move. By this time, the insider transactions showing heavy insider purchases are printed in the *Wall Street Journal* and elsewhere. Now the institutional investors begin to sit up and take notice. At least six institutions that sold the stock on the way down start buying it back on the way up, at about the same prices at which they sold.

To shorten the story, about a year later the cut dividend is increased back to the original level, and reports of higher earnings begin to appear. Another dividend hike follows, perhaps nine months later, and as the stock's uptrend begins to accelerate, acquisitions are announced, pushing the stock still higher and making room for still higher reported earnings. Suddenly, one day in the insider transactions reports, the names of the same insiders who bought at the bottom appear as sellers. Wall Street has become very bullish on the stock. But lo and behold, the company reports lower earnings just when everyone was calling the stock a long-term growth situation! The price plunges, etc., etc.

The manipulators of financial news are not always subtle in their attempts to mislead the public. There have been instances in recent years where corporate officials have talked to the press about products that never even existed—or if they did exist, they were nowhere near being salable, such as one company's new color camera that was supposed to out-Polaroid Polaroid, and another company's remarkable new glass product that would serve as both a window and a room heater, and still another company's Indonesian offshore oil discoveries, to say nothing of still another company's alleged cancer cure.

These are but a few instances where hundreds of investors were misled into buying a stock on the spectacular prospects of new products that were purely imaginary, or really not new at all, or completely impractical and ridiculous.

What to Ignore in the Daily Financial Section

For obvious reasons, newspapers have a vested interest in the idea that the stock market moves up or down because of things that are happening in the news. Thus we often read, in the financial section, that the market went down yesterday because President Nixon said such and such, or that the market went up because the head of the Federal Reserve Board said such and such, or that concern over the situation in Greece made investors nervous and therefore prices slid, or that enthusiasm over the latest peace overture in Southeast Asia encouraged traders to buy, and therefore prices rose.

Newspaper publishers obviously want people to think that they have to read the newspapers in order to know what stocks are going to do. But the truth is that the daily news has only very temporary effects, if any at all, on the stock market. For every instance of war news making the market go down, I can find one of the same kind of news making the market go up. Peace has made the market go both down and up. So has increased government spending. So has decreased government spending. Even inflation has made the market go both up and down. The market, in short, tends to be a kind of closed system, tends to follow its own laws of physics, as it were. When the market is ready to go up, any news at all will "make" it go up. When it is ready to go down, any news will "make" it go down. If a stock, or stock group, is in a strong uptrend, bad news will usually only stop the uptrend for a few days, or at most a few weeks. When a stock or group of stocks is in a downtrend, good news about the stock or stock group will push it up, but only for a few days or so. The most successful traders and investors are more or less unmoved by daily news developments. They keep their eye on the ball—the ball, in this case, being the basic trend of their stocks, and the real, fundamental worth of each stock they follow. To do this, they look for things that indicate what is really going on in the market, or in individual companies. These indicators are generally hidden from the view of the typical newspaper reader—and, for that matter, of the typical newspaper writer.

What Did the Market Do Yesterday?

Most people answer this question by saying, "It went up three points," or "It went down a fraction of a point," referring to the net change in the Dow Jones Industrial Average, the most widely-watched indicator of market action. And because the DJIA is made up of thirty large corporations, all of them widely-held issues, the DJIA usually does what the market as a whole does, so that the net change in the average usually describes the overall net change in stock prices.

There are periods, however, when the DJIA's action diverges markedly from that of the overall market. For example, during 1967 and 1968, the DJIA was far outpaced by the Standard & Poor's 425 Industrials Index as well as by the New York Stock Exchange's index of all listed stocks. Both of the latter, broader-based averages moved way up into new high territory, while the DJIA failed to penetrate its early 1966 high.

There were two main reasons for the lack of unanimity among these averages. One was that the 1967–68 period was the tail end of history's longest and biggest bull market ever. During the final stages of a bull market, the more speculative stocks—the cats and dogs—always outperform the investment grade issues, such as the 30 Dow Jones Industrials. The other was that the DJIA is weighted on the side of cyclical stocks rather than growth stocks, and after the long bull market of the '50s and '60s, the possibility of rapid growth had become the sole criteria for many institutional investors. Finally, as we saw in the previous chapter, a great many performance-minded institutions were concentrating on smaller, newer companies, where the various types of "instant performance" described in Chapter 2 were available. During the 1969–70 bear market, the Dow Jones Industrials, needless to say, held up a little better than did the rest of the market.

When you look at the financial section to find out at a glance what happened yesterday in the market, you really need to glance at a number of things beside the DJIA or the other averages. You should look at the number of advances and declines among listed stocks—these figures are usually included in every summary report of the market—to see if a divergence appeared between the net change in the averages and the advance-decline figures. Usually on a day when the averages rise, the number of advances exceeds the number of declines. Sometimes, however, the averages are artificially bent one way or another by a big move in one of the heavily-weighted stocks, while the majority of issues went the other way. The averages are all weighted in favor of the biggest companies with the largest number of shares outstanding.

Also, you should look at the number of stocks that recorded new highs for the year and the number of lows. This also tells you how strong or weak the market's action yesterday was. In addition, it is often a good idea to have your own average of "key stocks" that tend to show what the big traders have been doing. For example, during the 1960's, Polaroid was a favorite of the traders. As a result, it often tipped the market's hand, moving up a day before the market started up, or selling off a day before the market started down. So, to get a further insight into what is going on in the market, glance at several of the glamour stocks that have been trading favorites recently. If the averages went up yesterday but the trading favorites went down, there may be cause for near-term caution. For a full discussion of indicators of market action, see Chapter 8.

How to Apply the Theory of Contrary Opinion

It is by now a well-documented fact that at key turning points in the stock market's history, most predictions are wrong. Even the experts, at these times, are usually mistaken in their assessments of both the market and the economy.

After the 25 percent decline in stock prices in 1946, Congress launched an investigation of market letters to determine whether the "sell" recommendations of advisory services were responsible for the decline. To their astonishment, they found almost no sell recommendations in the hundreds of letters they surveyed. Moreover, at least 80 percent of the services were decidedly bullish, right at the market's peak.

Back in 1949, when history's longest and steepest bull market was first getting underway, more than 80 percent of all of the economists, market analysts, security analysts, financial writers and brokers were bearish. At that time, the DJIA was a bargain-basement 160. In early 1966, when the same average hovered near 1,000, over 80 percent of the same kinds of experts were bullish. (A decline of 250 points followed, hitting bottom in October 1966, when almost everyone had finally turned bearish.)

Between the extremes of 1949 and 1966, there were many other examples of how wrong the opinions of investors are when they are nearly unanimous, as they are at important turning points. One notable example was the situation that existed in late 1957 and early 1958, when the DJIA was down in the low 400's and the gloom was thick. The ratio of short interest * to average daily trading volume reached an unusually high 2.58, indicating widespread bearishness and pessimism. What followed was one of the broadest and sharpest advances on record, with the DJIA rising more than 50 percent in less than a year and a half.

When the bull market of the '50s and '60s reached its final "blow-off" stage in 1968, it was impossible to find a genuinely bearish analyst on the Street.

The Theory of Contrary Opinion, whose principal advocate has been an investment advisor named Humphrey Neill, is a theory that the best road to profits is to adopt the opposite point of view from that of the crowd whenever the crowd is nearly unanimous. It is really just an attempt to capitalize on the tendency of nearly everyone to be wrong about the stock market. However, most people who have based their investment decisions

---

* Total number of listed shares sold short.

on this theory have also been wrong most of the time! *The trick is in knowing when to become contrary.*

To know when to become contrary, you also have to keep in mind the old slogan, "Never fight the tape." This slogan means that when you see a trend unfolding, whether you agree with it or approve of it or not, you have to go along with it. In a sense, this principle is almost diametrically opposed to that of contrary opinion. But it is true that people who attempt to make trading profits by being contrary often end up fighting the tape. You cannot get anywhere by being contrary all the time. You have to wait until a trend has unfolded, and opinions have finally become almost unanimous. Then you can go against the crowd and your chances will be pretty good.

A key test you can use to determine whether it is time to become contrary is whether or not there are still a lot of people who are skeptical of the current trend. When Polaroid, Xerox, Control Data, and other glamour stocks of the 1960's began their long, meteoric rises, there were plenty of skeptics pooh-poohing the ridiculously high price/earnings ratios and the widespread public enthusiasm for these issues. In part, this skepticism could be seen in the short-interest figures, which were very high throughout the rise in each case.

But as these stocks continue to fool the bears and keep going higher, they begin to look more respectable as investment vehicles. Even the big New York banks began buying them for their common trust acounts, and some of the biggest universities began selling more conservative investments, such as American Telephone & Telegraph, in order to buy more IBM, Xerox, Polaroid, Burroughs, Control Data, and the like. The ranks of the skeptics have gradually thinned out. Opinion is nearly unanimous that these are virtually perpetual growth situations that would always have high P/E ratios that could be counted on to go higher every year, even in market declines. *That sounds a bit like the time to become contrary* and sell these stocks short!

The same idea holds true for stocks that have been going down and down and down, amid widespread bearishness. You can't buy them until the downtrend has gone much too far and reached a point where just about everyone has given up hope that the stocks will ever go up again. When the public has lost all interest and opinion is almost unanimously negative, *that is the time to become contrary and buy for the long haul.*

QUESTIONS AND ANSWERS

Q. What is your opinion of investment clubs?

A. I'm not too keen on them. Any group of people attempting to come to a group decision about the stock market tends to be wrong more often than an individual coming to a decision by himself. I can't really explain why, but this is a phenomenon that has been noted quite often. Moreover, investment clubs, like any other business venture, occasionally fail altogether. According to the National Association of Investment Clubs, this happens most often during the first year of the club's existence. On the other hand, the famous Mutual Fund Investment Club of Detroit is well into its fourth decade of operation.

Index

Index